Guardian Angel
911

J.T.Glisson

The Florida Historical Society Press

Guardian Angel 911

Published by the Florida Historical Society Press (2005)

ISBN: 1-886104-19-0

The Florida Historical Society Press
435 Brevard Avenue
Cocoa, FL 32922
www.floridabooks.net

To

The Shriners of North America

ACKNOWLEDGMENTS

I wish to thank my dear friend, Lucille Higham (Aunt Ciel), from whom I unconsciously cloned the personality of my guardian angel; Lorry Roess for her magnificent editing; the inventor of the spell check, the only barriers between me and illiteracy. Robby Roess for keeping the machine operational; Pat and Paul Roberts for their authoritative council; my son, Father Nicholas, who feels free to criticize any of my work from the pulpit; my sister, Marjorie, who is an inclusive part of this narrative; along with my middle-aged young'uns, who are an enduring source of encouragement and pride. And especially my wife, Pat, without whom nothing happens.

Cover and Illustrations J.T.Glisson
Guardian Angel Drawings Patricia Apone Glisson

PREFACE

This book is not intended to be a sequel to my book *The Creek* (1994, University of Florida Press). I have conscientiously avoided the assumption that the reader is familiar with *The Creek*, therefore where there is duplication I offer my sincerest apology.

Not unlike all our lives this book is a series of stories, separate but interconnected. They are all true with the exception of some literary license where details were lost in the telling and retelling. *Guardian Angel 911* will provide an insight to the sojourn of a native, born in the isolated hammocks and swamps of the real Florida, before the population exploded in the third quarter of the twentieth century. It is a trek that ultimately extended across three continents, but in reality I never left the home.

I was born at Cross Creek, (locally called, "The Creek") because my folks migrating from Georgia, missed a road and ended up there by accident. My parents found their place in the world. And for three quarters of a century it was the ideal place for me to launch my worldly expeditions. In addition to my Cross Creek family, I had another family five hundred miles to the north. That family was at the Shriners Hospital for Crippled Children in Greenville, South Carolina. A birth defect resulting in extremely clubbed feet, made it necessary for me to spend three to six months of each year at the hospital, beginning when I was five months old and continuing until my ninth year. It was at the hospital that I learned there were churches other than Methodist and Baptist, and was introduced to such outlandish things as cauliflower, mineral oil, wicker furniture, and stuffed olives. Everyone was kind and generous. The Shriners straightened my clubbed feet and made it possible for me to walk. The hospital also taught me about man's love and compassion for his fellow man and inspired an unquenchable thirst for the exciting world waiting just beyond the horizon. I shall always be grateful to the Shriners. Like hundreds of thousands of other children they gave me the opportunity to be and do the things one dreams of.

There was other factors that influenced my expectations: my special friends at Cross Creek, my neighbors, and especially Marjorie Kinnan Rawlings. She was my next-door neighbor, (if one can consider two hundred yards next door). Miz Rawlings was easy to talk to, kind and understanding. She could be a perfect lady if that included having an explosive temper as big as her heart. I was surprised when she wrote the classic, *The Yearling*. I couldn't believe she could know the intimate thoughts of a twelve year old. In my teenage world it was the ultimate adventure. Her book, *Cross Creek*, was about the place and the people that lived there. She described my family and me. I thought she did good job. The critics agreed.

Although capricious and occasionally volatile, Miz Rawlings was my buddy and advisor. My dad said in matters pertaining to me, she was more like a co-conspirator.

The years I spent writing *The Creek*, a chronicle of a place and time, were happy years. It was like going back and reliving my childhood.

This book is also about remembering the years that followed my growing up at Cross Creek. My father told me the night before his death, "Son, life is like taking a trip on a train. It's a one-way trip. Sit up, look out the window and try not to miss anything. You take my advice and enjoy the ride." Although I was young then and not too prone to take advice, I was deeply moved by what he said and made a vow not to miss anything. By writing this book I have been forced to admit my trip on this earth could have been very short, except for an extraordinary rear guard, named Lucille.

FOREWORD

When I first came to Tampa in 1984, I knew very little about the cultural and historical resources of the state or its history. Like so many "emigrés," I knew about Disney in Orlando, the large cities like Tampa, Miami, and Jacksonville, and a little bit about Tallahassee. I knew about Gainesville and the University of Florida by virtue of my affiliation with the University of Georgia and the Southeastern Conference. I also knew where Kissimmee was simply because a young classmate of mine in Homerville (Georgia) Elementary School had once lived there, and I, along with my less-than-worldly friends, took a perverse delight in teasing him about "Kiss-uh-me?"

One of the earliest acquaintances I made in Tampa was a young graduate student at the University of South Florida, Millie St. Julian. Millie, who also worked for the Florida Endowment for the Humanities, was very well informed about craftsmen, artists and writers in the state. One of the people she thought was an "unexploited" cultural resource was this tall, lanky resident of Cross Creek named J. T. (Jake) Glisson. "You really must meet him," she insisted. "He was the prototype for Jody in *The Yearling*."

Since one of my favorite books, borrowed over and over again from the bookmobile that traveled the dusty roads of Clinch County, Georgia, was *The Yearling*, I couldn't pass up such an opportunity. My first meeting with Jake was a phenomenal experience—unusual in the sense that it seemed that we had been neighbors and friends for a lifetime. Unusual, also, because we had so many-shared experiences that only people who grew up in the rural isolation of a southern state knew. We could talk endlessly about "rolling stores," kerosene lamps, "light'erd wood" and neighborhood characters. Everything seemed to be the same microcosm separated, not by time or age difference, but by the geographic quirk of a couple of hundred miles. His life foundation was the same foundation for mine. His experiences were my experiences. Kindred spirits united in an appreciation for the places and people who "reared" us.

An accomplished artist and designer, Jake once informed me that he had designed the "double-wide" and manufactured the first double-wide mobile homes that dot the rural South. Perhaps this is the only real bone of contention that ever surfaced between Jake and me. Having spent countless hours driving rural two-lane roads behind trucks pulling these weaving behemoths at excessive speeds on the straight-a-ways and then creeping at a snail's pace in corners, I had developed an intense hatred for these monsters. My irritation was mitigated somewhat when Jake explained that he invented them and didn't drive the trucks that pulled them, and, he said with that crooked grin that lights up his eyes, "Nick, they do serve a real purpose." Mitigated, perhaps, but in the back of my mind there is still a sneaking suspicion that somehow J.T. is at fault.

As he and I became closer friends, Jake regaled me with his recollections about his close neighbor and friend, "Miz Rawlings." His accounts of her life in Cross Creek and the relationships she had with her neighbors brought forth gales of laughter and mirthful tears. A consummate storyteller, he could create visual pictures of this famous literary giant engaged in the most human activities, taking time from her busy schedule of writing to weigh in on issues of importance to the residents of Cross Creek, and to exchange barbs with those that displeased her. "Jake," I frequently urged him, "you've got to write all of these stories down."

Out of this collection of stories came Jake's first book, *The Creek*. I'd like to think that I was responsible for that, but I know that countless other friends had been encouraging him also. *The Creek* was a wonderful addition to Florida literature. Jake proved he was as adept with a pen as he was with an artist's brush—a worthy successor to Rawlings as Cross Creek's leading literary figure. Even now, some five years after it was first published, I occasionally pick up *The Creek*, select a chapter, and get a quick spiritual uplift. It is that kind of book!

After *The Creek*, Jake produced a one-man play entitled *Sigsbee*, which his friend, actor Rip Torn, has optioned for presentation on Broadway. Sigsbee Scruggs was the Gainesville attorney who represented Rawlings in her famous court trial. Once again, Jake showed a great versatility in both writing style and subject matter.

Now he has done it again. In this latest effort, Jake provides an autobiographical look at his life, the people he has encountered, and, perhaps with a bow to some form of eastern mysticism, to "Lucille," the guardian angel who has tended to take a large role in the progress of his life. Given Jake's restless nature and his penchant for doing the unusual, combined with a large dash of irrepressibility, Lucille certainly has had her work cut out for her. Even the assistance of "Miz Pat," Jake's tolerant and forgiving wife, has done little to lessen the burden for Lucille. I do not know if there is any kind of relief available for guardian angels!

I invite you to read this book and to enjoy its many facets. Not only is it an autobiography, but it also provides a guide of "how-not-to" live your life. On the other hand, I cannot see how Jake would have become Jake without the ameliorating effects of these adventures of body and spirit. I certainly look forward to the next product of the fertile mind of one of Florida's greatest literary figures!

Nick Wynne

Chapter 1

LUCILLE

I have never been visited by creatures from outer space or seen a flying saucer. As a matter of fact, I don't believe in ghosts on Halloween, or little elves that live in the woods. I believed in Santa Clause when I was a young'un, and then reversed the hoax on my parents in an effort to keep the presents coming after I learned better. My dad brought that to an abrupt end with one of his jewels of wisdom, "Son, when you start thinking about courtin', you're too big for Santa Claus."

Mythical figures provide us with a lot of fun, not to mention considerable profit. Nevertheless, I do believe in gallstones, the IRS, and guardian angels. One of my aunts had several gallstones in an olive jar on her mantel and most of my friends have had encounters of the third kind with the IRS. Guardian angels are not so commonly acknowledged. Most people believe they had one in the past but have trouble believing she is still around. If I tell the truth, I can't say I have ever seen one, but as sure as a skunk has body odor, I've got a guardian angel. I cannot remember when she first made her presence known. It was probably when I was a young'un napping and yawning in the old Baptist Church in the village of Island Grove, or possibly during one of the spirituals Aunt Martha's sang while she worked in momma's kitchen. Nevertheless, I liked the idea. Angels could fly anywhere and were so pure they didn't need to take baths. It seemed reasonable to me that guardian angels would be assigned at birth. However one should not be picky in matters of such ethereal origin. My guardian's presence was very real to me when I was a little young'un and she still is.

Recently, I met two practicing psychiatrists at a social event and realized personal angels were tricky subjects. I learned it is all right to acknowledge you think you have one, but never, never, never should you ever admit talking to one, or that an angel spoke directly to you. It is easy to get a padded room with no furniture if one confesses to having conversations with anything invisible. There is an old saying, "Familiarity breeds contempt." It also reduces formality. During my growing up years, maybe thirteen or fourteen, I became uncomfortable addressing her as Guardian Angel. It seemed much too formal, especially at the Creek. I thought about it and asked her to give me a sign. Immediately a name popped into my mind. I said out loud, "You have got to be kidding!" and broke up laughing.

She responded by causing me to experience a shortage of breath. I said, "Your name is *Lucille*?" I could not help it, I laughed again. "What kind of angel would be named Lucille?" I continued to laugh. That was when I nearly choked to death. Since then her name has been Lucille. I call her Lucille and I don't make jokes about her name anymore.

I do not want to give the impression that our relationship was always sweet and rosy. When I was a young'un, I was frequently mad at her. I would do something wrong and get caught, causing me to send out an urgent request to have Lucille blank out my parents minds on the entire matter. As an alternative I would suggest she make me some kind of a hero by twisting the facts around a little. The answer was always the same. Guardian angels, and especially Lucille, didn't interfere in family affairs.

After I had been properly punished I wanted to forget the whole matter and forgave everyone including Lucille. I didn't have enough friends to go around burning any bridges. All things considered, my relationship with Lucille was more like that with an older sister than with someone from the supernatural. Of course, I felt over-blessed. I already had an older sister.

There were times when I wanted to say, "Shoo, Lucille! Go away. Get!" In my teens I began to think of her like a brat who insisted on tagging along. Occasionally she made me downright uncomfortable. This was particularly true when I was with my buddies or on the rare occasions when I was around a real girl. Although the last soul I wanted to think of on such a grand occasion was Lucille, she would force her way into my mind, sowing words like "honor, gentleman, respect."

My thoughts were, "This ain't no place for a lady! Scram!"

Ten years ago she zapped me with a thought, "You are the most ungrateful, reckless, selfish human I could possibly have been assigned to. I have pulled you out of all sorts of mayhem and what do I get?" She always answers her own questions. "I occasionally get a quick thanks a few seconds after the fact when you are sure you are not dead or crippled for life."

She was on a roll, and continued, "I should be proclaimed a hero. Instead, you forget the whole thing until the next time you need me. I can't remember a single time you looked up and said, 'Thanks for Lucille. She is doing a great job down here.' Any other Master of Angels but mine would have recalled your angel years ago."

When I thought about it, I was sure she had been requesting transfers for years. I could easily imagine the bureaucratic form: Request for Transfer. Name: Angel Lucille, Profession: Guardian Angel, Client: J.T. (the jerk) Glisson,

Length of Current Assignment: More than a half century, too long. Reason for this Request: Chronic fatigue, occupational stress, post hazard depression, ruffled feathers syndrome. Personal Comments: Why, O why me? My friends say I look like a road-killed bag lady. Take back the wings. Every time a bell rings, I lose a feather. I can't take it any more.

All this couldn't have come at a worse time. I am getting older, my eyesight ain't what it used to be, my bones are getting brittle, and I don't react like I used to. The bottom line is, I'm scared Lucille will quit and leave me to look out for myself. I don't know if a person gets another angel when his angel quits. If they do, I would probably get a young one that is picky and scared of her own shadow.

Desperate times call for desperate measures. I tried to reason with Lucille for weeks. She finally said she might reconsider if I made some changes and showed proper gratitude for everything in the past. I hate to bow and scrape but there is no point in fishing after the pond goes dry. I told her I had already started to change and would drown her in a sea of Cracker gratitude. She said I didn't have to be dramatic, just thank her for every single incident in which she had pulled my ungrateful rear out of the fire.

She then spoke calmly (something I didn't know she could do), "You thank me properly and start listening to me before you jump into your stupid escapades or I am out of here." Her last words were, "I want it in writing." I considered her ultimatum and decided, since I am a man of towering honor, not to mention deep-in-debt when it comes to gratitude, that I would review all the incidents that occurred during the past forty years, especially the more outstanding predicaments for which Lucille demanded gratitude. With considerable effort, I have documented each situation where she appears to have interceded on my behalf, with the hope she will sign on with me for the rest of this worldly expedition.

Chapter 2

THE QUEST FOR A GUARDIAN ANGEL

Airplanes have always been a part of my imagination, my dreams, and ambitions. I love airplanes. I drew pictures of them before I started to school and showed them to my philosopher friend, Henry, and to commercial fishermen at Cross Creek where I grew up.

When the first murmurs of one of those magnificent flying machines came over the horizon, I frequently courted punishment, racing out of the house to identify it, and to marvel at the pilot up there where there were no rules or schools or things to do. I usually saluted, in the event he was looking down. On more than one occasion, I dashed from the outhouse, ill prepared to run or have any social contact with a pilot or any other living being.

There was only one plane that was a familiar sight at the Creek. It was a bi-wing Stearman piloted by a man who lived somewhere west of Orange Lake. My friend Bernie, who knew a lot about everything, said somebody said the pilot's name was Boots.

Boots flew the local crop duster out of any place he could find that had a hundred and fifty yards of fairly level dirt. He was naturally the most famous pilot in our area mostly because he was the only pilot, and because he had walked away from more crashes then he could count. Folks at Cross Creek admired that. The crashes were not Boots' fault. I think that if they had crash inspectors back then, the crashes would have been classified "farmer's error." The farmers would forget to tell Boots they had left a tall fence post in the middle of a cornfield, or that they had borrowed some of Boots' gas to go in the family pickup.

When he went in (crash-landed), Boots did the repairs and inspection at the crash site while his injuries healed. And when the old biplane was air-worthy, he would back up to the fence and fly out of the field and resume crop dusting.

I was about fourteen the first time I saw Boots flying over Big Hammock Grove, three miles from my home. He skimmed down the lanes of trees with his fixed landing gear inches off the foliage. At the end of a row, he would open the throttle, pull the nose up with a mighty roar, roll into a sharp banking turn, then throttle back and slip down to dust the next row.

All I could see from our place was the plane shooting up at the end of the rows with the engine echoing across the lakes and swamps, then dropping back below the tree line. The sight of an airplane cutting such didos at Cross Creek was unbearable. I abandoned the weeds I was suppose to hoe from my momma's garden and took off in that direction.

A passing car gave me a ride part of the way. Then I cut through the hammock guided by the sound of the engine. Exhausted, I ran out of the woods into the clearing of the grove in time to see him zoom past, sitting high in the cockpit wearing goggles and a leather helmet. He looked in my direction and gave me a thumbs-up salute. For me, that moment will always be right up there with the time Miz Rawlings hit Mr. Brice's mule and the lift-off of Apollo XIII.

Although it meant neglecting the work I was supposed to be doing, I went to the grove every time he dusted. Then one afternoon, Boots suddenly set down at the back edge of the grove and rolled to a stop. I ran through sand spurs waist high to meet the pilot and touch a real airplane. In spite of being out of breath I told him, "Mr. Boots, I am J.T. and I am going to be a pilot."

He spit tobacco juice on one of the tires. "The way I calculate it you already got a lot o' aircraft observing time logged with me and this old mule."

Throughout the summer I flagged and marked rows and helped with anything I could on the ground when Boots dusted the Big Hammock Grove. I wanted to ask him to teach me to fly but was afraid he would laugh at such a silly notion. Then out of the blue, he said, "Looks like I might as well show you how to fly this mule before you steal one and get yourself killed." I stood with my mouth down around my knees. "You get over to my field across the lake Saturday and we'll have at it."

I told him, "Yes sir, Mr. Boots. You can bet on it. I am gonna be there if I have to swim Orange Lake to do it." He said, "If we are going to be flying together, I 'spect you better call me Boots. It'll make it easier to communicate."

To my surprise, my dad didn't object when I told him I wanted to be a pilot. He said he guessed flying would be like driving when I was grown, so I might as well get at it. Dad took me over to Boots' field and left when the pilot said he would drop me off back at the grove.

I waited while Boots tightened a wire wing strut and parked his pick-up in the shade. At that moment he looked twenty feet tall even though he was slightly shorter than my dad. He was definitely overweight around the middle but was obviously strong and muscular. With the exception of the skin around his eyes, which was whiter than the rest of his face, his skin was tanned the color of his helmet. I supposed it was from wearing goggles. He had khaki trousers and a faded khaki shirt and wore dust-caked pilot boots that came half way to his knees.

Boots came over and addressed me with a tone of rehearsed authority, "Well, J.T., I can't teach you nothin' about flying in and out of fancy airports, you'll have to get that from this book." He handed me a grease-stained student manual that had been folded down to pocket size. He slapped the fabric on the side of the fuselage with his glove, "What I will teach you is how to fly one of these mules without it killing you. The reason I call all aeroplanes mules is, don't you ever for one second ferget it's waitin' for its chance to kill you. If you got a problem with one, put it on the ground and then deal with it. You listen to me and you should be able to fly until you are a hundred." He turned toward the plane then turned back, "J.T., you got a guardian angel?" I stuttered, "I guess so." He said, "If you ain't got one, get one. Th' time will come when you will need one." After that, guardian angel Lucille's presence became a part of my life. Boots put on his leather helmet and goggles, and threw down into the cockpit a flat, worn pillow that separated his rear from the metal seat. I wondered if his momma made the pillow for him. It was red and had tassels on it. He said, "Now, after we do our preflight check, I'm gonna fly you around and let your stomach get used to floating up and down. An' while we are up there, I'm gonna show you something I plan for you to remember the rest of your natural life." Boots made me personally put my hand on everything involved in the preflight check and repeat the purpose for inspecting it. When we had finished, he climbed in the cockpit and told me to get in and sit on his lap. While I squeezed in he said, "It's a good thing you're skinny or I would have to give up half my belly to get you in." He mumbled something about it would be good to have two cockpits but this was the way he had learned to fly. The rest of what he was saying was lost in the smoke and noise of the radial engine roaring into life. In seconds we were in the air. I was flying in a fabric covered relic out over the lake and Miz Rawlings' house, as well as the house where I lived and was born.

At that moment the world changed for me. It looked different, like a model or a picture, clean and beautiful. We flew south, past Ocala to a hill that was unusually high for Florida. There was a gash cut across a pasture. Boots pulled back on the throttle and nosed down in a glide until we were one hundred feet off the ground. Boots pointed to a path of debris strewn across the field and a wing with N numbers (civilian aircraft identification numbers), separated from the other wreckage. Boots leaned forward and yelled into my ear, "A man and his wife got killed there night before last. Their mule got 'em."

I yelled, "Why?"

He yelled, "Weather? Mechanical?" He shook his head. "It's too late to ask why."

We circled the wreckage two times then made a direct flyover. Boots waggled the wings but didn't look down. While flying back from the crash site, he let me hold the stick and ride the foot rudders on top of his boots. We made some lazy turns and I tried to keep the nose level with the horizon. When we were over Orange Lake, he took the controls, pulled the nose up, then cut the engine and glided in without power, rolling to the exact spot where he always parked at the grove. I climbed out breathless and tired. Boots was looking down at his instrument panel and, without looking up, he said, "You did fine, J. T. If the weather is good we will do it again next Saturday."

He fired the engine and flew out in the direction of his field.

Several months passed before I took off alone and flew that dust-covered relic out over the lake and Ms. Rawlings' house and the house where I was born and lived. I followed the creek to Lochloosa where my friends and I fished and ran from the game wardens. I looked down at a pair of eagles circling over the lake. Some stayed at the Creek year around and some migrated beyond the horizon to places I had only dreamed of. I, too, could stay at the Creek or I could fly beyond the horizon. I decided I was going to be pilot and fly for the rest of my life. Flying forever was an exciting thought, but it sure was lonely up there. I found myself talking to myself and, at times, it was scary, especially when I came in too fast to land and was not able to see ahead when the tail was down. Boots was right, but first I needed to improve my relations with my guardian angel to avoid being a part of the wreckage strewn over some unnamed field.

Motivation is an elusive urge. Hunger, sex and fear of falling all come naturally, but motivation sneaks out when you least expect it. Motivation is not necessarily good. It occasionally leads to disaster. There were many sound reasons why I might have lived out my life without piloting an airplane—the Depression, money and opportunity. However, the author of Jonathan Livingston Seagull said it best, "Be careful what you pray for, you will probably get it."

My quest for a guardian angel began with my mother, since she was the authority at our house on church, the *Bible* and things like that. I asked her if everybody had a guardian angel.

She thought about it and said, "I think young'uns' mothers are their guardian angels when they are little. Mothers look out for them and protect them from all of the things that could do them harm until they get big enough to be out on their own." She sat thinking for a few moments and continued, "I am sure that everybody that is of age has a guardian angel. Some people calls it conscience and intuition, but there is more to it than just that. Sometimes something just rears up and says, 'look out, there is danger.'" She nodded her head up and down, "Once you start thinking about it, the more you'll be convince you've got a guardian angel." She laughed, "They're supposed to be all hes, but mine always seemed like a she," and went back to her cooking.

I decided getting to know my guardian angel was going to take some time and a lot of thinking.

Chapter 3

HOKKAIDO

In August 1945, they dropped the bomb and World War II ended as abruptly as it had begun. I suppose I was typical of soldiers at that time, although most would later claim they understood the concept of the A-bomb. All I knew about atoms was from an article in a 1936 fourth-grade *Weekly Reader* about a cyclotron that could split an atom. It didn't say why anyone would want to split an atom, so my knowledge of nuclear physics ended before it began.

I will always remember the evening of August 6, 1945. I was returning to my quarters from the flight line when my buddy, Bob Hager from Illinois, yelled, "Hey, Glisson. Did you know the war is about to end?"

I said I didn't and asked, "Why?"

"Because we dropped a bomb on them that was so big it wiped out a whole city."

The next day everyone was talking about a B-29 destroying Nagasaki with a second A-bomb. I couldn't conceive of anything so powerful, but if the army said it was so, I supposed it was so. The war was over.

Everyone in the Pacific assumed they would be a part of the invasion of Japan, followed by a hell of a battle. We expected that fight to last until the last Jap was defeated. Then, and only then, would the survivors be allowed to go home. That was not to be. Within hours after the second bomb, we were on our way to the Japanese homeland.

There was nothing in our training about occupation. I didn't know what occupation was, having come from Cross Creek only a few short months before. However, that was of no importance. My brief Army Air Corps training had taught me to do what I was told when there was no alternative, and not to try to anticipate what the army would do next.

We landed at Iramagowa, a Japanese air base just outside Tokyo, in the usual confusion that was typical of the military. Overnight, Iramagowa became Johnson Field and the Fourth Replacement Depot for the Fifth Air Force. Everyone was reclassified and assigned to units of the occupation.

With some manipulation on our part, my buddy, Hager, and I managed to get classified together and shipped to Chitose Army Air Base on the island of Hokkaido. I asked my new Commanding Officer, "Where is Hokkaido?"

"It's a wilderness island as far north of here as you can go and still be in Japan," he answered without enthusiasm.

His first sergeant spit in a northerly direction and said, "Gonna be colder than a well digger's butt up there."

Lucille shivered, "I don't like cold weather, J.T. We should have stayed in Florida." It would be almost impossible to get any farther from Cross Creek geographically or culturally than Hokkaido. I didn't even know what Japan was like and certainly nothing of the customs and history of the Orient. After three days on the world's slowest train, we arrived at Chitose. The former Japanese Navy Air Base had been one of their best, strategically located for the northern defense of the Islands.

My commanding officer summoned me to his quarters and gave me what was the most loose-ended general order any soldier ever received, "Glisson, as of now, you are responsible for anything that occurs outside the perimeter of this base that does, or could, negatively affect the base or its personnel. All of the men here came into the service to win the war and that has been accomplished. And although I don't want them to know it, I do not expect to have a single man held over here one day longer than necessary because of some infraction or mishap with the Japanese. Is that clear?"

I snapped, "Yes, sir!"

He continued, "The 49th Fighter Squadron was the best fighter squadron in the Army Air Corps and will continue to be." He paused and then said softly, "If something comes up, take care of it. Understand?"

I said, "Yes, sir." It seemed the proper time, so I asked if I could have my buddy, Hager, as a partner.

The colonel said, "It's done," and dismissed me.

A jeep was permanently assigned to me along with an oversupply of firearms. Hager found a room on the second floor of a building located a half-mile from the area where most of the men were quartered. With a little ingenuity, we acquired two hospital beds that adjusted to any position the occupant desired, and had curtains made from parachutes to give our new quarters a feeling of home.

In the first days of the occupation, no one knew how the Japanese would react to the sudden loss of the war or the occupation of their homeland. Caution was the order of the day, until it became apparent the Japanese were more concerned with avoiding starvation and getting on with their lives, than with any retaliation.

The first morning after Hager and I secured our quarters, we set out to reconnoiter our new domain. The Island of Hokkaido was much larger than I thought. It had mountains, magnificent forests, the city of Sapporo (later occupied by the 77th Infantry Division), and a sprinkling of small towns and villages. I couldn't believe the beauty of the unspoiled forest, pristine lakes and crystal clear rivers. There was a serene magnificence unlike the riotous, fast-growing subtropical forest I was familiar with in Florida. Two majestic mountains stood tall above the horizon south of the base. One retained the perfect cone-shaped symmetry of its volcanic origin and remained snow capped ten months of the year. The other, a few miles to the east, was marked by a lazy stream of steam drifting up from its volcanic core. I told Hager we were going to climb that mountain before we left Hokkaido. He agreed.

We studied maps at night and explored the far reaches of the island from dawn to dusk. Frequently, we stayed overnight in private homes when the distance was too great to cover in a single day. We tried to learn Japanese, but mostly depended on my drawing pictures to communicate.

When I was a young 'un growing up at Cross Creek, Miz Rawlings gave me a subscription to *National Geographic*. It was the only publication we received and would have been my favorite if we had dozens. Each month when it arrived, I would lie on the floor studying the nooks and crannies of the wondrous world that lay beyond the Creek, while my parents protested my staying up too late. I decided when I had the opportunity, I would explore *National Geographic*'s world. Hokkaido seemed as good a place as any to start.

The base bulletin board carried duty rosters as well as Occupation Information that set the rules of conduct for all military personnel. Some bulletins restricted military personnel from consuming Japanese food, which was in extremely short supply. Others forbade patronizing houses of prostitution.

One morning a particular bulletin buried beneath the jungle of paper caught my eye. It discouraged fraternization with Ainu natives. The mimeographed bulletin described them as aboriginal Caucasian people who were the original inhabitants of the islands of Japan, prior to the ancestors of the present-day Japanese who migrated from the mainland of Asia. I was amazed to read that the Ainu were similar to the American Indians. They had their own culture and language. The bulletin pointed out that any contact with the Ainu was unlikely since they lived secluded in the forest of Hokkaido.

I was fascinated by such people. I told my buddy I wanted to meet some if we ever got the opportunity.

He said, "Glisson, we haven't learned enough Japanese to ask directions to the toilet. What are you going to do when you meet some wild man out in the forest?"

I told him, "You are talking to the United States Army Air Corps' most qualified specialist when it comes to talking to people from the back-woods."

Building a boat occupied our attention for the next four weeks. We scrounged materials any place we could find them. I told Hager the boat would give us an opportunity to explore the rivers and shoot ducks. He explained he didn't have any experience with boats. I said, "Hager, old buddy, that is no problem. I'll teach you when we get it in the water." We christened the boat the *Water Bucket,* named after the *Air Bucket,* a tired old C-47 everyone used to get their minimum flying time in.

We launched the boat, with a one-plane flyover and a lot of beer, into a small stream that ran parallel to the base. While Lucille mumbled something about Hokkaido not being like Cross Creek, and why didn't I play poker in a nice warm room like all the other soldiers, Hager interrupted, "When are you going to give me that lesson in boating?"

I told him, "As soon as we cast off. You can't teach boating on dry land."

The current was swift and we were suddenly flying downstream. In a few minutes, we were further down than we had ever been. Hager, fresh from the flatlands of Illinois, and I, used to the lazy streams of Florida, had no experience with swift current. We lost our paddle and began to face the fact that we couldn't stop.

The Japanese who lived alongside the stream were cheering and waving as we flew past (or that is what we thought they were doing). One threw a rope, Hager caught it and damn near pulled the old man in before he could turn it loose.

A few minutes later, we learned they were trying to tell us there was a low bridge ahead. We zipped around a curve and found ourselves hurtling toward a footbridge only an inch lower than the sides of our boat. We both jumped overboard. The boat crashed into some pilings beneath the bridge and swung crosswise to the stream. We scrambled up on the sinking boat and onto the bridge.

Hager said, "Glisson, is there anything else you think I should know about boating?"

The Bucket was hauled out from under the bridge with the help of several Japanese and some strong ropes. The damage was extensive but after several days work, the boat was like new again.

As usual Hager had to insert a little Illinois humor, "It's like I always say, Glisson. You got to expect losses."

Our next expeditions were more successful. We frequently saw large flocks of ducks on the rivers. I told Hager, "I am a duck hunter and we are going to have a duck dinner." He was a little reluctant but agreed to go along after I told him we would borrow two shotguns from the MPs and shoot the ducks as we floated down the relatively slow stream.

We improvised a rack to carry the boat on our jeep and were on our way before sunup the following morning. A friend of ours from Georgia, nicknamed Tank, came along to return the Jeep. After picking our way through the forest parallel to the Chitose River for two hours, we arrived at a point several miles upstream. Tank helped us to carry the boat and shotguns down a fifty-yard sloping embankment, and launch it in the river.

While we unloaded the boat, I had the feeling that we were being watched, but was unable to see anyone. Lucille and Hager and I shoved off and spotted our first flock of ducks around the first bend in the river. We lay low in the boat drifting until we were only a few yards from the ducks, then raised up and shot them on the wing. Long shots were impossible because of the short barrels on the riot guns. We killed several in the first flock, then came upon one flock after another.

On one occasion, two birds floated into some brush near the bank, making it necessary to go back and retrieve them. I walked back along the narrow bank to the place I was sure they had lodged but could not find them. I had never seen any turtles in the river and knew they didn't have any 'gators in Hokkaido to steal my duck for its dinner.

Then I found a fresh human track in the sand near the place they had lodged. It was not the Japanese thong-type sandal, but rounded on the edges with no heel, like a moccasin. I looked and called, but all I could hear was Hager bailing the boat downstream. He was not impressed by my imaginary duck thief and was anxious to continue the hunt.

We killed all the ducks we wanted and drifted the last two or three miles without shooting more. The men of the Chitose Army Air base had a splendid duck dinner that night courtesy of the Glisson and Hager expedition. Even Lucille approved. We repeated the river duck hunt two more times before the winter set in and the snow became too deep for the Jeep. Winter in Hokkaido seemed to last forever. The base was snowed in during January and February, and nothing other than planes on the flight line moved in or out.

I tried to learn to ski and darn near killed myself. Hager became pretty good at it and went on daily cross-country ski jaunts while I stayed penned up on the base. One Sunday morning, I saw Tank driving an army-tracked vehicle called a weasel. He was towing a bunch of men out to the ski run. I was inspired with what I thought was a great idea, or at least it seemed so at the moment.

The river was swifter than it was during the summer and had not frozen except along the edges. We could take ol' *Bucket* up the river with the weasel and come back downstream to Chitose. Hager said, "What for?" I told him we would fish for trout and maybe get some ducks that hadn't gone south. As usual, he reluctantly agreed and Lucille objected.

The next morning we dressed in our warmest gear. I picked up the shotguns from the MPs while Hager procured shells from the ammunition dump. I greased my battered fishing pole and laid in a supply of k-rations. We put *Bucket* on Tank's weasel and moved out. Snow had fallen all night, stopping just before daylight. The sky was clear, illuminated with sunshine worthy of our Florida winters. Powdered snow kicked up behind the weasel, sprinkling minute ice crystals in the morning sun. I felt great to be out doing something and enjoying the anticipation of a new adventure. We moved effortlessly over the snow, arriving at the place where we had previously launched the boat, sooner than I expected.

Everything looked different. The river was much higher and swifter than it had been in the fall. Ice extended out from the banks thirty feet, leaving only half the river's width navigable. The slope leading down was covered with snow and much too steep for the weasel to traverse.

Hager said, "Glisson, do you want to back out?"

I told him I wished he hadn't put it that way. If we could get out into the river, we could go downstream the way we had planned. *Bucket* had a sheet metal bottom and would slide easily on the snow and ice.

I don't remember who suggested we get in the boat and slide down the slope to gain enough momentum to cross the ice into the river. I am afraid it was me and there is one thing I am sure of-Lucille objected loud and clear.

Sliding down did sound logical. In fact, I believed it would work. Tank kept racing his engine, said he had to get back and pull some skiers to the run. I asked Hager what he thought. He said it made as much sense as the other things we did.

We barely got the boat off the weasel before Tank headed back to the base, and I had the feeling that someone was watching us the same as I had back in the summer. We loaded our gear in the center of the boat. Hager got in the front while I held it in place. The plan was to let it slide as fast as it would go while I dug the paddle in the snow like a rudder, forcing the boat to hit the river bow first.

My guardian angel spoke emphatically, "Don't do it, J.T.! Don't!"

Hager said, "Glisson, what are you waiting for?"

I said, "Nothing," and shoved off. I have no doubt John R. Hager and J.T. Glisson set a downhill bobsled record that morning, worthy of international acclaim. As to any control, I had absolutely none. We reached the ice over the river before I could sit down in the boat. The only thing that happened crossing the ice was a ninety-degree turn of the boat causing us to hit the river broadside.

Hager was thrown out on impact. The boat and I went down together. I came up trying to cling to it like I was taught back at the Creek. That was no problem because my foot was caught under the middle seat. Although the river was freezing cold, my first concerns were to free my foot and save the shotguns.

I passed beneath a small tree hanging out over the water and grabbed onto a limb. The weight of the boat being pulled by the current was so strong that I could not hold onto the tree. I knew I was in trouble. The current and the ice extending out from the banks would make it impossible to get out. My only hope was to find a log or something extending out into the river strong enough to pull myself up onto the ice and then slither my way to the shore.

My strength was exhausted, leaving me no choice but to release the tree and hope to get my foot loose as I drifted downstream. At the same moment I released my hold on the tree, a long dugout canoe glided within inches of my face. I grabbed the side and looked up at the man controlling the canoe. He was handling it with a long pole like the Seminoles in the Everglades. When the speed of the canoe was equal to the speed of the sunken boat, I kicked my leg free. My wet clothes made it impossible to climb into the canoe until he ran the bow up onto the ice, allowing me to slither into the dugout. The craft was so narrow I was forced to lie prone on the bottom to avoid turning it over while my rescuer raced further downstream and picked up Hager. My buddy's balance was worse than mine, making it necessary for both of us to lie flat on the bottom, feet-to-feet. Even though I was freezing, I thought we must have looked like a Cross Creek gator hunter coming home with two six-footers.

With expert mastery, the boatman poled us back upstream past the place we had launched Bucket, and then a half mile further to an island in the center of the river. When we stood up, our clothes were frozen stiff. Our rescuer led us to a round, thatched structure about sixteen feet in diameter that looked from the outside like a smooth dome-like mound in the snow, with a trail of smoke coming from the center.

We stepped down past more than two feet of ice and entered through a narrow doorway covered with a rough piece of fabric. The minute we were inside, the man motioned for us to remove our wet clothes. It was dark with the only light coming from a small fire located on a mound in the center, and a smoke hole in the roof directly above it.

We were both blue. Any place I was not numb, I felt like a thousand pins were pricking my skin. We didn't argue. When we were naked, he gave us a soft fur skin, which I believe was a bear hide. He motioned for us to lie down and roll up in the skin and we responded without question. He then put some liquid into a pot and placed it over the fire. Our teeth were still chattering when he offered us a tin cup, and with a positive gesture, motioned us to drink. I have no idea what it was, but it was warm and produced a glow throughout my body. I reckoned it was Hokkaido's version of Big Scrub moonshine.

In a few minutes, I was warm and my eyes became accustomed to the dim light. The walls were black from years of smoke and for the first time, I realized there were other people in the hut in addition to our rescuer—a woman, a small girl maybe ten or eleven, and a little boy who appeared to be just walking.

At the Creek, we would call him a yard young 'un. He tried to probe at the fire with a stick, but his mother admonished him in a voice that was not audible. Obediently, he nestled beside her.

The girl was wrapped in what appeared to be a dark gray blanket. Her eyes were shockingly large, staring in our direction, but focused on the space a few feet in front of where we lay. I was mesmerized by her large eyes until I remembered I had become accustomed to the squint of the Oriental children.

I thought it was the absence of light at first glance, but then there was no doubt, the skin around the woman's mouth was black. I wondered if it was some kind of makeup or perhaps medicine. She had black hair, heavy eyebrows and black eyes. Although she was not pretty by any western standard, she looked gentle and reflected a wisdom that could have originated in a cave, eons ago.

The three sat without sound or movement staring straight ahead. They were like wild animals I have seen clinging together waiting for some instinctive signal to tell them what to do.

I lay there thinking how different their lives were, and was envious of their knowledge and understanding of this place on the other side the world from my home at the Creek. Our rescuer left the hut without notice, leaving nothing but silence. Exhausted, I slipped into a deep sleep.

Soft humming awakened me, and I spent more than a few seconds deciding where I was and how I got there. The woman was fussing over a pot, obviously cooking something. The odor reminded me that I was hungry. Hager was sitting up trying to hide his nakedness with the skin our host had given him. He looked around and spotted our clothes hanging from the ceiling twelve feet over our heads. I had no idea how they got up there or how we would retrieve them.

Hager moved closer to me and whispered, "Glisson, this is a hell of a situation. There ain't no toilet in here and I need to go and all our clothes are hanging up there on the roof." He paused choosing his words, "We may have got naked in front of the man's wife and children when we came in, but I sure as hell don't plan on doing it again." I suggested he keep the fur skin rapped around him and run outside.

He said, "I am sorry I asked. And what do you think I will use for paper?"

When I said, "Snow," I believe he would have hit me if he could have, without dropping the skin. Then he took a deep breath, jumped up, and ran out the little door like a frightened rabbit with the bearskin covering part of his rear.

The man stood up across the room surprised by the sudden retreat of my friend. I pointed to my groin area. He almost smiled. I moved closer to the fire preserving as much modesty as possible, then pointed toward our clothes, indicating I wanted them. He made a wringing motion and shook his head no. I assumed they were still wet. Hager came running back in and squatted behind me.

He said, "Glisson, it's cold as glory out there. I almost fell in the river again."

Our host spoke to his wife. It was the first time since he pulled us from the river he had spoken to anyone. His voice was soft and positive. It could have been a Carolinian accent if one didn't try to understand the individual words. The language was clearly not Japanese. The wife put some thick soup that was almost stew, into deep wooden bowls, then handed them to us along with sets of chopsticks. I don't know if it was because I was so hungry, but I thought it tasted great.

Taller than the average Japanese, the man had wide shoulders, a long torso and short legs. I was fascinated by the way he scanned the room by slowly moving his eyes without turning his head. I decided he was like the fishermen back home, shy and gentle, but capable of putting up a hell of a fight when it was necessary. His eyes were squinted similar to the Japanese but with the glare of the snow eight months out of the year it was no surprise. We tried speaking to him in English and our skimpy Japanese. If he understood us, he didn't acknowledge it. The woman retreated back against the wall and squatted near the sleeping children.

It was a strange circumstance. The man had saved our lives. I never felt more gratitude or a greater need to express it, but we couldn't speak to them. We couldn't give them anything. We were naked.

I told Hager that maybe we should tell him our names. He tried, pointing to himself saying "Hager", then pointing to me and saying "Glisson." There was the slightest indication of a nod, nothing more. His expression was neither friendly nor hostile. He appeared to be a man accustomed to dealing with any situation that arose, including two foreign soldiers that fell in his river.

I was sure our host was one of the Ainus. I pointed at him and said, "Nippon?" He nodded no. I pronounced Ainu as close as I could imitate in Cracker English, enunciating, "I-New?" With a slight movement of his head he indicated yes.

Hager said, "He is not much of a talker."

Dawn began to lighten the sky through the smoke hole in the roof, and our rescuer took a pole and retrieved our clothes. I held Hager's bear skin while he put on his trousers. He in turn held mine. The woman retrieved our socks from her bosom, warm and dry, and handed them to her husband. He in turn handed them to us, along with our boots oiled and dry.

Our Ainu host offered more soup and we declined. Then I was astonished when he ducked outside and returned with our side arms and both shot guns.

Hager said, "So that is where he went after he brought us here."

I agreed but could not imagine how he retrieved the guns from the river, especially in the near darkness. I tried to give him one of the shotguns but he motioned as if he was pushing me away.

When we were outside, he called to his wife. She came to the door, bowed Japanese style, and smiled. He also smiled for the first time since we met and led the way across a foot log to the south bank of the river. I wondered whether he was indicating he was glad to be getting rid of us, or that friendliness was only shown outside his home.

Clouds had returned, but thankfully there was no wind. Hager and I fell in line behind our rescuer who was clearly still in charge. We followed obediently as he trudged through the snow moving parallel to the river in the direction of Chitose. We had only gone a half-mile when we heard a plane coming in our direction. With unbelievable speed, our Ainu leader pulled a white cloth out of his shirt and squatted in the snow covering himself. The P-51 buzzed over us and was gone seconds later. He put the cloth back in his shirt and moved on as if nothing had happened. I couldn't believe how quickly he had camouflaged himself. I wondered if he knew the war was over or didn't want his presence known to any strangers. One thing was clear. I knew then how he had taken the two ducks and disappeared so quickly.

After trudging another mile, I heard the familiar sound of a army weasel coming in our direction. We ran ahead waving until Tank saw us and roared up within inches of where we were standing. We went through the usual soldier's greetings, "Hey ol' buddy," and, "Are you guys lost again?"

Tank said, "When you fellows didn't come in last night, I figured something went wrong and started looking first thing this morning. Went up the other side of the river, couldn't find you, then tried this side. I asked one of your buddies to see if he could spot you in the Grasshopper, but he must of decided to use a P-51. Wasted his time. Too fast."

I looked around to introduce our Ainu friend. He was gone.

Hager said, "Glisson, that guy is like a mouse. He disappears every time you move."

I asked Tank, "Did you see our Ainu buddy who was in back of us?"

Tank asked, "Who?"

Throughout the rest of winter, I thought about the Ainu family huddled together in their thatched house set on an island in the Chitose River. I wondered how long they had been there and how long the mountains and the forest could exclude them from the rest of the world. I later learned, from an anthropologist who had been a professor at the University of Sapporo, that the family I had happened upon was one of the last of their race. The black area around the woman's mouth was tattooed there when she took a husband and lost her virginity. The Ainus were the hairiest people on earth with a culture and a religion unique to their race. He said that anthropologists disagree on their origin, and that some consider Ainus a race without a history, living their last moments before extinction.

Less than one hundred Ainus survive today. The anthropologist said that the end of the war would bring about the need for forest products and more space for the Japanese people. The remaining Ainu would be forced to assimilate, even though their blood would be considered inferior.

Spring was glorious in Hokkaido. The snow that averaged thirty-six inches melted suddenly, opening the roads to all the places on the island we had missed in the fall. A Japanese fish hatchery found our boat twelve miles downstream and returned it several weeks after I kicked free of it in the river. Hager and I found new rivers to explore and climbed the mountain east of the base.

Even though we were going from morning to night, I frequently found myself thinking about the little Ainu family. I decided to pay them one last visit before we shipped out for home. Hager and I collected some simple gifts that would possibly make their lives easier. A hatchet, an ax, and a small sewing machine similar to the hand cranked ones used by the Seminoles back in Florida.

We drove the jeep as far as we could and hiked the ten or twelve miles to the Island. The change in landscape was unbelievable. The landmarks I had become familiar with were lost in the vibrant green foliage. We followed the south bank of the river as closely as possible in that we could see only a few feet ahead.

When we were in what we believed was the vicinity of the hut, the foliage became even heavier. We stopped occasionally and listened for sounds that would reveal the location of the hut without success.

Hager joked, "Glisson, what is the difference between being lost and not knowing where we are?" I told him I knew where I was, I just didn't know where the rest of the world was.

The trail turned suddenly, and we found ourselves at the end of the foot log leading to the island and the Ainu hut. The little girl we had met before was on the center of the log carrying a basket of white flower blossoms picked without stems. She was coming in our direction.

I will never forget the look of absolute terror on her face when she saw us. She threw her hands up in a protective gesture spilling part of the camellia-like blossoms. Then like a wild deer, she jumped into the shallow stream, running for her life, strewing the remaining flowers as she ran. She did not scream, but made a guttural sound that could be heard even after she climbed the bank and disappeared in the brush.

Hager and I stood mesmerized, watching the delicate blossoms floating beneath the log until the last floated past. I felt a deep sense of shame, but didn't understand why.

Even though there was a trickle of smoke coming from the hut we decided not to disturb them any further. We set the gifts on the log and walked silently back to the jeep.

There were a thousand questions I would have liked to ask the man who pulled us from the Chitose River, but I knew I would never have the opportunity. The extinction of a race, and the dissolution of a place is a sad commentary on human wisdom.

Hager and I agreed we would not tell our buddies on the base about the unique family in the forest. The impact of hundreds of curious, well-meaning soldiers would most surely hasten their extinction. Thanks to Lucille, we had the good fortune to glimpse a beautiful and vanishing world and survive.

Chapter 4

GIRLS & GROCERIES

When Lucille and I were discharged from the Air Corps following World War II, I did not know what I wanted to do in the near future; more importantly, I didn't know what I wanted to do with my life. The only profitable business venture I had been associated with was a partnership with a renegade hog named Blue and her pig production. That business had been when I was in high school and was concluded suddenly when my sow laid siege on all the Creek, chasing the fishermen's dogs, and feasting on their fish before they could be sold. My father closed it shortly after the three-hundred-pound hog was caught breaking and entering a tenant house, and subsequently wrecking the place.

There were several things I positively didn't want to do. After growing up chasing my dad's scrub cows in the swamps and marshes, raising livestock was the first occupation on my "don't want to do" list. Being a responsible young man, I tried systematically to consider those things I liked best. That was easy-girls and food.

No sooner had I conceived that enlightening revelation than my brother, Carlton, asked me if I would like to go into the grocery business with him. I asked, "Where?" He said he thought Lake Wales was a nice town. I thought it was a great choice also because I had toured the state and concluded there were more pretty girls per square inch in Lake Wales than any other place in Florida. In addition, everybody had to eat groceries. You couldn't have a better combination than that.

I committed my army severance pay (twelve hundred dollars) to becoming a merchant in that beautiful, south-central Florida town. When I told my father I was going into the grocery business in Lake Wales, he pressed his lips together tight and looked down at the ground.

"All you boys know about the grocery business is eating 'em." He looked past me, studying the sky above my head. "I wish you luck." He then looked straight at me. "Call me when you start going under. Before you go too deep in debt, I'll buy you out." He turned and got in his pickup and drove off toward the bridge.

I was infuriated. My father had the audacity to prophesy failure before I started! Who was he to predict failure to a noble business located in a prosperous town a hundred miles from the Creek? And to add to the insult, Lucille agreed with him. I was angry and hurt by my father's lack of confidence, and ignored Lucille.

My vision of the future of the business was clear—I would make buckets full of money, date the town's most prominent girls, and join the Jaycees. I caught a ride to Island Grove, boarded a Greyhound bus and was off to seek my fortune in the world of produce, meats and canned goods.

Looking back, I can see a close similarity to Steve Martin's role in *The Jerk*. My experience building fishermen's shanties, along with my brother's similar skills, was put to immediate use building the store. I thought the location was perfect. It was in the middle of town, between the old Walesbuilt Hotel, and a family who owned a sheet metal shop. The metal shop owner had two beautiful daughters, so this was a perfect location.

Two months later, we had a grand opening. Lots of people came, read the labels on the cans, squeezed the produce, and bought a quart of milk. Pretty girls came into the store, but I had no time to notice. I was too busy mopping floors, picking up trash, and, mostly, culling rotten tomatoes, gushy cantaloupes, corn worms, and black bananas with yellow spots. At closing time, nine p.m., I was too tired to have noticed Marilyn Monroe in a skimpy bikini.

We never made expenses. There was cost of power, cost of transportation, taxes, equipment payments, meat spoilage, produce spoilage (vegetable and fruit fondled to death by ladies fulfilling some subliminal urge). Our business predated Saran Wrap, so the steaks went from bright red to a rigor mortis gray in twenty-four hours. On the bright side, we ate a lot of gray steaks. The late '40s was the drive-in era, a time when wheels were more important than looks. I didn't have either. Our only transportation was a ton-and-a-half truck, bought to haul produce from Tampa. It soon became apparent that pretty girls didn't go to drive-ins in produce trucks.

My enthusiasm for the grocery business was waning at an alarming rate, when my army buddy from Illinois came roaring into town in a new straight-eight Pontiac sedan. I was never more delighted to see anyone and especially Bob Hager with his super wheels. I asked the girls from the sheet metal shop for a date and was surprised when they said yes. One of the girl's girlfriends later told my brother that my date accepted only "to prove that looks were not important."

Although we dragged Main, coasted up Spook Hill, and walked around Bok Tower holding hands, the metal shop owner's daughters were not impressed. I thought something more dynamic would win them over, and made a suggestion I would later regret. "Why don't we go to Cypress Gardens tomorrow!"

The Sheet Metal sisters of Lake Wales beamed with excitement. One said, "That would be perfectly mar'rr-velous." Her sister giggled and fluttered her eyelashes at Hager.

After we dropped them off at the sheet metal shop, Hager said, "What and where is Cypress Gardens"?

I told him, even though I had never been there, I understood it was a tourist attraction that had pretty girls and pretty flowers in a swamp that bordered a sand-bottom lake.

He said, "And Glisson, you are telling me people pay to get in a place like that?" I told him we could probably go swimming there, and more importantly, the girls would be impressed.

We picked up our dates who were wearing pink-and-green checked-gingham sun dresses, two sizes too small, both cut low in front and back, with sun hats made of the same material. I was reminded of a phrase, something about "my cups runneth over," and one I made up myself, "tight in all the right places and loose where it counts." I was impressed.

The girls had neglected to bring their swimsuits, but Hager and I had brought ours along just the same. For the first time since I had gotten into the store business, and although I knew it was losing more each day, I was determined to enjoy the moment. I conjured up an image of a successful young businessman, a Jaycee-type, and led the way into the Gardens.

The place was then, and still is, magnificent—fantastic flowers, waterways, ancient cypresses, and beautiful girls strolling about in antebellum gowns. We ambled through a sea of flowers, past orange and yellow flame vines, and beneath crimson bougainvillea cascading from the tops of ancient pines.

I was reveling in the grandeur of the moment, when one of Lake Wales' town sports saw us, and came strutting in our direction. I could not think of anyone I cared to see less than that dude, and especially at that particular moment. He was one of the regulars who stopped by the store every evening to buy Sen-Sen (a breath freshener) and brag about his exploits with the local women.

"Well, well! Did y'all just bump into each other or did y'all come together?" he asked. Then he spoke in a stage whisper directly to my date, "If I had known you would like to come over here, I would have been glad to bring you myself."

She giggled and said, "That would be fuuunn."

At that moment, the public address system that had been playing in the background was interrupted by an announcement, "The world famous Cypress Gardens Water Ski Show will began in ten minutes." We, along with five hundred other tourists in the Gardens moved like dairy cows at milking time to the edge of the lake and settled on a manicured carpet of grass overlooking the ski area. Even though it was obvious there was no public swimming, Hager and I both still carried our swimsuits.

The intrusive dude made sure he sat next to my date. The sound system picked up John Philip Sousa's "The Thunderer," promoting an atmosphere of cultured anticipation.

A well-dressed, expansively casual man picked his way through the crowd, speaking to everyone as he passed, until he was standing directly in front of us. He spoke to the five of us simultaneously, "Are you folks enjoying the Gardens?" The dude said he especially liked the pretty girls, gesturing back toward the gardens.

The stranger addressed Hager and me, "I see you fellows brought your bathing suits. By any chance do you water ski?"

Something about being ignorant and thinking tourists swam at Cypress Gardens, coupled with standing tall in front of the dude and the girls, caused me to do something even I would not believe.

I said, "Yes, me and my buddy ski all the time."

The gentleman in front of us smiled, "That is wonderful. I am Dick Pope, the owner of Cypress Gardens. We are always glad to have our guests participate in the show. Gentlemen, if you will go right up the path here to the locker room, you can put on your suits and pick up a pair of skis."

I heard Lucille shouting, "No! Apologize and back out now!"

The dude said, "I shore am glad to meet you, Mister Pope. My friends here will put on a show everybody is gonna remember."

I motioned Hager toward the locker room. He had a look of utter amazement on his face. He knew I had never been on water skis in my life. He pointed out, "Glisson, you never made it down the hill once on snow skis when we were in Japan without breaking or cutting something."

I said, "You did, and you have water skied before."

He snapped back, "I tried to learn to water ski in Illinois and only got up once for a short distance before I fell."

I said, "OK, we'll go to the locker room and out the back door. Let the dude take the girls home."

Behind us Dick Pope called, "Young men, just a minute. I want you to meet my son, Dick Pope Junior. He is the only man in the world that skis on his bare feet." The handsome young man moved next to his father.

We mumbled, "How do you do?"

Mister Pope addressed his son, "Take these men to the locker room and get them a pair of skis. They are going to ski in the beginning of the show."

My date jumped up squealing, "Oh this is soooo exciting!" She gave me a spontaneous hug and a quick peck on the cheek. Young Pope told us to follow him, explaining, the show was about to start.

The band music, the powerful speedboats warming up and the electricity of the crowd drowned out Lucille's screaming: "No. You fool! Don't do it. No!"

Young Pope handed each of us a pair of Cypress Gardens skis. I knew when we undressed and put our clothes in a locker we were committed.

Hager whispered, "Glisson, you have got to be crazy. What are you going to do out there on skis at fifty miles an hour, write an instruction book? Why don't you be the second man to ski barefoot while you are at it?"

I told him he sounded like Lucille. He said, "Who?"

We had covered each other's rears all through service. I don't know if he had an angel yelling at him, but I did know he wouldn't back out on me. We followed Dick Pope Junior back through the mass of people still gathering to see the show. Young Pope asked if we wanted to take off from the dock chairs or from the water.

Before I could answer, Hager said, "The water." Then he turned to me and whispered, "Keep the points of the skis together and out of the water. If we are lucky, I'll see you in the emergency room."

The boat sat blubbering only a few feet away while the driver threw out two coils of rope attached on one end to the boat. He then pitched the end with the handles to us. Lucille was screaming, while the boat motor made a high-pitched sound like drag racers waiting for the green light.

I heard the master of ceremonies saying, "Ladies and gentlemen, as special guests of Cypress Gardens, we have a native Floridian and his friend from the great state of Illinois to start off the show." The pull boat roared to a screaming pitch and sped toward the center of the lake.

The rope made a swishing sound coming out of the water following the boat. I thought, "What the hell, I might be a natural at skiing and amaze everyone." The line tightened, then jerked forward. It was like going up Niagara Falls in flood season. I tried to hold on. The skis were all over the place. I truly didn't know which way was up. The skis came to the surface for a second, before one flipped on top and then over the rope, swinging me around backwards with the handle across my pelvis, and the rope coming out between my legs.

I was screaming "L-U-C-I-L-L-E!" while I inhaled gallons of water.

Finally, Lucille rolled me free and off the rope.

I thought how nice it would be to drown right there. Then I realized Lucille would save me again. Being pumped out was the only thing that could be more embarrassing.

The following morning, I was once again on a Greyhound headed back to Cross Creek, while Lucille sulked somewhere in the back of the bus. Being sore and bruised all over was bad enough, but the memory of having that obnoxious little town dude helping me to the car, and then traipsing off with the giggling sheet-metal sisters, was more than I could bear. Even my buddy Hager couldn't wait to get back to Illinois and left before daylight. I was content to wallow in self-pity for the first hundred miles. Then my Angel Lucille came forward and started into her how-many-times-do-I-have-to-tell-you routine. And then she said, "You have a total disrespect for intelligence. I am going to ask for a transfer."

I resolved to give up groceries and girls (temporarily). I thought of the quiet beauty of sunrises on Lochloosa, the pungent odor of the hammocks, and lines of white ibis drawing the curtain on another day at the Creek. I thought, "I'll go fishing with Bernie. Then I will look into a new profession."

C-LISSON

Chapter 5

THE ROAD GANG

Following my abortive career in the grocery business, Lucille became a veritable nag. "What you need is a profession, a low-risk career, something safe," she said at least ten times a day. My momma said it twice a day.

And once a week, my dad said, "Son, why don't you go into the cow business?"

My current girlfriend became like a phonograph needle stuck in a groove, "You would never believe how successful my brother and all my old friends are. They are all successful. You know, J.T., success. That is what really counts." She sounded more and more like Lucille, so I wished her success and looked for another girl.

In the fall of that year, I enrolled in refresher courses for veterans at the University of Florida. I worked part-time for the gas company, cleaning machinery and picking up coal that spilled in the yard.

My old car gave up the ghost and died in front of a funeral home in Gainesville. It seemed as appropriate a place as any, so I removed the license plate and left the clunker there. Two blocks down the street, I bought a bicycle with no fenders. The bike provided satisfactory transportation, except on rainy days when the water sprayed up from the tires and wet me on the underside. In addition, the bicycle brought about a new revelation—girls don't go with a man whose only transportation is on two wheels.

The spring semester ended while I foundered along. I felt a deep yearning to do something, pursue a profession, but I didn't have the slightest idea what. College was O.K., but I had no concept of what I should major in when I returned to the University in the fall.

I was leaving campus when a classmate, Clyde Coleman from Milton, Florida, said, "Glisson, what are you doing this summer?" I admitted I didn't really know. He smiled like a used car salesman when a customer reaches for his wallet, "Why don't you come with me and operate a big powerful earth-moving machine?"

He looked over his shoulder toward the north, which I assumed indicated the direction of the big machines, "My daddy has got a highway construction company and if I recommend you, he'll give you a job. You can run a bulldozer or a crane." I told him I didn't know how to run a bulldozer. His enthusiasm was not dampened. "That's no problem. You know how to fly and run a farm tractor. Bulldozers are somewhere in the middle. I'll teach you."

I said O.K. before Lucille had a chance to object.

The next morning found me back on a Greyhound, on my way to seek my fortune in another profession for the second time. Lucille was in a pessimistic mood. There was something about bus stations, crying babies, and the smell of alcohol-saturated passengers that always put her in a mean mood. Lucille hissed, "You know, if we stayed at Cross Creek this summer, you could have slept under clean, sun-dried sheets and eaten that marvelous food your mother prepares."

She was getting wound up. She did an instant recall of the Lake Wales grocery fiasco, then reached way back and brought up my gator-hatching business back when I was still a kid. I told her to go sit with one of the drunks in the back of the bus.

Clyde was waiting for me at the Sinclair station and bus stop in Wewahitchka (referred to locally as "We-wa"), when I got off the three o'clock bus from Tallahassee. "Welcome to We-wa, Glisson. I've got you room and board with a widow lady. She's got a son and a good-looking daughter. It's right up the road a little ways."

He grabbed my bag and threw it in the back of a pickup that I hoped wasn't his. "We've got to go out to the job first so I can teach you to run a Caterpillar-eight bulldozer before it gets dark." I tried to say something about my good clothes, but he continued before I could speak, "Then we'll take your things to your room." I climbed in the pickup and tried to find a space to sit among the Stillson wrenches and log chains.

Clyde took off before I could get the door closed. He drove the old pickup that looked like a survivor of D-Day, the way Miz Rawlings drove her Oldsmobile back at the Creek. The exhaust fumes caused my eyes to water, making it necessary to wipe them on my shirtsleeves. The whole time, Clyde shouted general instructions on the care and maintenance of bulldozers. I was absorbed, not by his teaching, but by the roar of the motor.

When we were on the longest, loneliest, straight stretch of road in West Florida, we met a car that was so dirty it was impossible to tell what brand or color it was. Clyde waved and hit the brakes, stopping in a cloud of burnt rubber, he executed a moonshine turn and speed-shifted in pursuit of the car we had just met. Speed was not necessary in that the dirty vehicle had skidded, leaving two black lines for thirty feet before pulling off the road.

Clyde jumped from the truck and ran to meet a stocky, near-fifty-years-old man charging towards him. They met like opposing linemen in the Superbowl, grabbed one another and wrestled to the ground. I jumped out of the truck with no idea of what was happening and stood bewildered, while they rolled over and over in the grass and sandspurs along the side of the road. The old combatant finally pinned my buddy and they both began to laugh. Clyde said, "I would have got you, Old Man, if I weren't afraid of hurting you." They embraced and beat one another on the back.

The older man felt Clyde's biceps like he was buying a horse, "You and who else? You're getting soft down there in college." He wiped his face and shaven head with an oversized bandanna, "It is good to have you back. I'll get you back in shape with some honest hard work this summer."

After Clyde and his dad dusted themselves off, Clyde said, "Dad, this is my friend and classmate, J.T. He is a pilot and a tractor operator from Cross Creek, down in Central Florida."

His dad looked at me for the first time, "He looks more like a backwoods Cracker to me." He gave me a quick smile that was intended to look phony. I thought I should take offense, but didn't know how to go about it. Mr. Coleman said, "See you in the morning on the job, six o'clock." I am sure my astonishment at the starting time caused him to add, "This ain't no damn university."

He jumped in his car and dug up grass until he was back on the pavement. Clyde yelled loud enough to upset the balance of nature, "YEEEHA! See, what did I tell you? Glisson, you got a job."

I said, "He didn't say that."

Clyde interrupted, "He would have said to get your butt down the road or something worse if he wasn't hiring you." He ran back to the truck with me trying to catch up. "We've got to hurry. I'm going to give you the shortest course in Caterpillar tractors and bulldozing in history." And he did!

Lucille complained, "This is going to be worse than water skiing."

I had watched 'dozers clearing land for my dad back at the Creek, but was not prepared for the magnitude of the machine when I climbed up into the operator's seat. The big machines were awesome. The steel track Caterpillar tractors were steered by clutches engaged with levers, and geared with several ratios of high and low ranges. Each tractor had a small gasoline motor to crank the enormous diesel engine.

I moved the machine around the yard until it was dark. Clyde said, "Glisson, you did just fine, but I think you should avoid working around the experienced operators, and especially my dad, until you've got a little experience." It was going to be like flying a new type of transport plane into a major airport with only a five-minute check ride for instruction.

We drove back to Wewahitchka at the same speed we left, though I didn't know why. Lucille sounded like an auctioneer above the roar of the engine and mud tires. She said, "Those things are dangerous even when someone knows what they are doing. Tell him no thank you and lets get out of here, now!"

I went to my room in a strange little town, in a strange house, and a strange bed. I believe it was the first time I knew loneliness. Lucille didn't seem to be around. I assumed she was off pouting or thinking up more reasons why I should have stayed at the Creek. I drifted off, thinking the machines were overwhelming, and my new boss was even more overpowering. But on the bright side, it would be something to chauffeur one of those monsters around.

Five o'clock is early anywhere, but it doesn't get earlier than it does in the West Florida backwoods. The company was building a road that would penetrate the massive Apalachicola River Swamp to the river. The job was ten hours a day, six days a week. Clyde picked me up and we arrived at the job site before sunup.

The men were all there, standing around drinking coffee from thermos bottles, waiting for six o'clock. Mister Coleman roared in bouncing over the rough ground and stopped inches from where we were standing. Being in such close proximity, I realized his car was a new Chevrolet, even though it looked like it had been the loser in a demolition derby. He got out and while all the men said, "Good morning, Boss," he ignored them and began directing each man to the specific job he wanted him to do. He also told them how long he expected it to take to do it.

He reminded me of General George Patton, or maybe Patton was similar to Clyde's father. If he had not had his head shaved, I am sure his hair would have been red. He had very light skin that had suffered constant exposure from the Florida sun, causing him to be what we called red-complected. His stocky build and stout neck reminded me of pictures of Napoleon without the high collar. After a brief consideration, I decided Napoleon would surely have cringed in Mr. Coleman's presence.

Boss Red, as I came to know him, gave the day's assignments to all the operators, then turned his attention to me and his son. "Clyde, you take the common labor crew and pick up the roots left in the right of way, pile and burn them." Clyde hesitated. His dad said, "Go! I want you to remember what this business is like from the ground up."

Then Boss Red turned to me, but Lucille spoke first, "Tell him we quit!"

I thought, "Why don't you tell him?"

He began, "Young fellow, I understand you got some instruction on operating my equipment yesterday so you are already in the hole to me several gallons of fuel, plus the wear and tear on the machine." He held up his hand as if I were going to protest. "Don't thank me. I'll take it all out of your pay."

He took a small notebook from his pocket and wrote in it while he talked, "You take that swing crane over there. Go down to the end of the grade where the right-of-way crew pushed down the trees and left the logs and stumps. Move all the logs and stumps out in the woods far enough they can't be seen." Then he added the clincher, "I doubt you can operate the machine or hold out doing a real man's work." He got in his car and went bouncing and sliding like a cartoon character back in the direction he had come.

The caterpillar was so ancient that the original chrome yellow paint had faded to a miserable tan color that had been spattered with dried mud and clay collected since it was new. A sixteen-foot steel boom pivoted from a cast-iron base over the center of the engine. The frame that supported the crane mechanism straddled the tractor, and was attached along both sides between the tracks. The old reprobate was smelly and greasy. I told Lucille it was much smaller than the one I had practiced on the day before and was probably safer.

She said, "It's a death trap."

I climbed up in the operator's seat, found the switch and turned it on, but I couldn't find the starter pedal. I looked on the floorboard in the place it had been located on the tractor Clyde had used to instruct me. There was no sign of a starter pedal in all the grease and dirt. I was desperate to get going before Boss Red came back and discovered I didn't know how to start the starter motor.

While I was looking for it, I discovered a pull rope in a tool compartment near the motor. I supposed the machine didn't have a starter pedal for the starter motor. I rapped the pull rope around the pulley and pulled. Nothing happened. I choked it and pulled the rope again. Nothing happened. It was hard to pull, but I persisted until I was exhausted. I pulled and looked up the road, expecting Boss or one of the other operators to appear any second. Finally, it stuttered and sputtered and cranked. I then engaged the big diesel. It turned over a couple of revolutions and roared into life.

I was overwhelmed with success, and floating in a sea of optimism. After following the rough right-of-way into the swamp for a half-mile, I reached the section where the trees had been bulldozed over and sawed into twenty-feet sections. By experimenting, I learned which lever made the boom raise up and down, which one made it swing around from side to side, as well as which one raised and lowered the cable with the hooks that attached to the log or stump.

After climbing down from the machine, I carried the thirty-pound hook and hooked it into one of the big logs. Then I climbed back up and pulled the lever that raised it high enough to make it possible to see beneath it, while I carried it to the woods. There was something manly about lifting the log with the touch of a lever and manipulating the machine, even though it acted more like a bucking horse tracking across the rough ground.

I told Lucille, "Look at me now. I'm a swing crane operator." She didn't answer. With a little effort, I maneuvered the tractor with the log out of the right-of-way. It seemed logical that I should place the log over to the side so I could come back to the same area with more logs. I swung the crane to the side, not comprehending that the tractor was very narrow in width, therefore not supportive to the sides, especially with a log that weighed two tons.

In addition, I had made a second mistake lifting the log up several feet from the ground. The machine promptly turned over sideways until the log struck the ground causing the hooks to release. With the weight gone, the tractor flipped back upright. The jolt was so severe, it threw me out of the seat and into the muck on the opposite side. I wasn't hurt, and fortunately no one saw what happened. Only my feelings were hurt, and my clothes were filthy.

Lucille said, "I see you now." She obviously had saved my neck but I was not about to admit it.

When lunchtime came, any strength I had was expended. And although I would have preferred to stay as far as possible from the other operators, I returned to the yard to eat my lunch and refuel. I parked away from the other men, but they all came over and introduced themselves. They were all thin, what we called wiry back at the Creek. They tussled and joked with one another as if they hadn't done anything all morning. Some were as old as my father. Frequently, I caught them looking at me as if they found me amusing. I wolfed down my baloney sandwiches and went to sleep sitting in the seat.

The hour lunch break was short. In what seemed like only ten minutes, one of the men woke me and said, "Little feller, I 'spect you oughter get your engine running so you're ready to get back to work when the time comes." I supposed being new made me a little feller, even though I was bigger than he was.

I got the starter rope and began to choke and pull, while they made suggestions of what technique might make it start. Eventually, it started, and I moved back to my assigned section to struggle with the stumps and logs for the final five hours of the ten-hour day.

I have never been as tired as I was when six o'clock came. I was so exhausted, it was necessary to let the tailgate down before I could get into the back of the pickup truck.

I ate, showered, and fell into bed. The clock rang and I caught the truck back to work. It was my total routine day after day, six days of the week. I was strong, young and healthy, but I was bushed at night. I turned down the operators' invitation to go juking at night, and slept all day Sundays. I could not understand why I was so tired. I would have loved to quit, but I was ashamed to give up.

In the military, I had actually enjoyed the rigors of basic training. Running the machine was hell. Lucille kept asking, "What are you trying to prove?" I honestly didn't know.

During the third week, it rained in the afternoon causing us to shut down. The operators were all gathered beneath a piece of canvas strung between two graders at the yard. Some were shooting craps while the others hunkered and talked about hunting, fishing, liquor, and women.

One of the older men sat looking at me as if he had something he wanted to say. After a couple of moments, he nodded to the other operators, and they in turn nodded. "Little feller, you look tired like a young'un raised without biscuits." He made a sucking sound and shook his head, "That tractor has just about got you whooped." I tried to deny it, but he continued, "If I was you, I'd clean all that dirt out of the floorboard of your swing crane. You can't imagine how much easier it'll make it run." The other men, including those shooting craps, agreed.

When the rain slacked, I thought, "Why not? It didn't make sense, but it would certainly be more comfortable. Using an old license tag, I scraped the sand and oily dirt out of the floorboard. While I was digging through the hardened goo, I bumped something and discovered a starter pedal, higher up beneath the dash than the area where I had previously looked. It was shiny, other than some newly formed specs of rust that had accumulated over the past three weeks. I turned the switch on and pressed the button. The starter rolled over and the engine sprang into life. I switched it off and was confronted with a loud cheer going up from the other operators and Lucille.

The tractor had a good starter. Like a fool, I had cranked it two times a day with a pull rope. The joke was on me. If I had asked, they would have told me. I considered whipping them all simultaneously and decided it would be easier to forgive them. In addition, the Boss came grinning over and gave me my first raise.

Naturally, the operators joked about how easy I started my engine the following morning. Then they told me I had passed their test and they had some advice for me. One said, "You are going to kill yourself if you don't let the machine do the work. You are tightening your muscles every time you turn the tractor. You push when you want to move over anything, and worse than that, you are straining when you lift with the crane. Let the machine do the work or it's going to work you to death."

I tried it that day and found they were right. I had been gritting my teeth and straining every muscle in my body when I maneuvered and lifted. That ten hours was easier than one hour the way I had been doing it.

Boss Red continued to demand the maximum effort from every man on the payroll. He told the operators, "The machine cost more and is worth more than you and your time, so I expect you to give 'em hell. Don't baby the bastards."

Each day we penetrated deeper into the swamp where the rich soil caused the trees to reach bigger and bigger proportions. The undergrowth was denser, and the muck and mud got softer. Boss gave me a man named Sam to hook the grappling hooks into the logs and stumps. We were soon working like a team. I put the hooks directly over the log. Sam was a lifetime friend of the boss' family, and the only black man on the job. He hooked the log and led the way into the woods spotting the best place to drop it. He referred to himself as "my hooker." It was several years later that it occurred to me, if he was my hooker, I would have had an unthinkable title.

The operators became friendly after their starter joke. When we gathered to eat or for payday, those who had been with the company for years told stories of how Boss had accomplished jobs that other contractors considered impossible. There was sincere admiration and respect for our hard pushing boss.

One of the older operators told me that during World War II, the U.S. government wanted to build airstrips on the northeast coast of South America. The plan was to ferry airplanes from there to Africa, via the Azores. The jungles of French Guyana triumphed over one contractor after the other. The older operator said, "Boss Red asked for the contract and told the government that he could do it. I don't think they believed he could, but they gave him the contract. Boss loaded his equipment on a ship and set sail. When we unloaded on a dock in Guyana, Boss Red told the ship's captain the exact day he wanted the ship to be at that dock to transport us back to the States." With pride in his voice, he said, "On the day Boss said for the ship to be there, we were waiting on the dock. That airstrip was complete and it was a good one. If Boss tells you something, you can depend on it."

Although I developed some skill, the work was still hard and Boss Red continued the pressure to move faster. The company received financial draws depending on the stages of completion. I agreed with Lucille that I didn't want to make a career as a tractor operator, but was proud I hadn't let it beat me.

In August, it rained several inches and delayed the work drastically. The rising level of water made it more and more difficult to work in the right-of-way, and particularly harder to dump the logs and stumps out in the swamp. Sam and I looked for any high places we could find to manipulate the swing crane without getting stuck.

On one occasion, I was surprised to find a Cracker shanty suspended on poles, ten feet or more off the ground, only twenty-five yards from the right of way. Sam said the shanty was up on poles because the river flooded nearly every year. He suspected its inhabitants fished and hunted and probably made a little 'shine. I had a feeling of shame for our invasion of their peace and tranquility. The noise of the machines was only the beginning of the sounds that would shatter their world. I thought it was ironic that I should end up at a place that was as isolated as Cross Creek.

Occasionally, I caught a glimpse of a large woman who appeared to be forty or fifty years old, peeping from the woods on the side where I had discovered the house on stilts. She obviously didn't want to be seen, so I told Sam I thought it would be best if we pretended we didn't see her. Each day she moved closer. She was wearing a dress made of cloth that appeared more like what had once been white canvas, not the kind of material women usually wear. She stood with her bare feet wide apart and her hands clasped behind her back. I could not decide if she was hostile or curious. Lucille seemed oblivious to the swamp lady's existence.

Unexpectedly, on a day when we were having our lunch in the area of the stilt house, the woman came out into the cleared right-of-way. She strode over the ground with unusual ease for a person sixty pounds overweight. She said, "Mister, I got a proposition fer you." Before I could answer she continued, "You bring me two cans of Railroad Snuff an I'll give you a quart of blackberries fer your trouble."

I asked, "Is the snuff for you?"

She said, "Who else? They ain't nobody else around here but me." She tilted her head to one side in a manner that indicated she was going to answer the questions I was thinking before I could get around to asking. "I got a husband. He's been gone a little over two years and won't be back fer another year. I live by fishing an' raising hogs in the woods, an' rendering soap from lard and ashes. I don't need nobody and like being by myself." She hesitated for the first time to catch her breath, "'Course, that's gonna change when that damn road comes through here."

I said, "Yes ma'am, I'll get your snuff."

She reached in her bosom and extracted a rag with some worn coins knotted in one corner, "You can bring my change with the snuff."

Sam grinned, "That lady shore knows another Cracker when she sees one."

I replied, "I would rather cross Boss Red than have a problem with that swamp lady."

The following day, I went through the strip of woods that separated the stilt house from the right-of-way, and came to a small damp sand yard that was swept clean of leaves and debris. A cone-shaped mound, with smoke trickling up from the center, stood on the backside almost beneath the house. I thought it must be the way she made ashes for the soap. Water oak, cut by someone obviously proficient with an ax, was neatly stacked beneath the house.

I called, "Hello."

The swamp lady pulled back a piece of burlap that covered the door directly over my head. She said, "I'm coming," and stepped out on the top wrung of the entrance ladder. She was directly over my head and started descending before I could discreetly look down and back away.

When she was on the ground, she moved closer than I was comfortable with, and handed me a quart jar filled with fresh blackberries. "Here is the berries. Picked them this mornin'." I gave her the two cans of snuff and turned to leave. She called to me, "Feller, you're welcome to come fer water, but tell them other folks I don't want them nosing around my place. Hits bad 'nuf having a damn road so close."

I said, "yes, ma'am," and went back to my machine.

When I got back to the crane, Sam grinned and said, "How come you didn't hold that ladder while that woman was getting down from her house?" I told him I was surprised he would spy on a poor old lady who only wanted a little snuff. He laughed and looked back over his shoulder, "You are the only man on this job that's seen the moon come up twice today."

The sun got hotter, Boss Red got tougher, and the mud got deeper each day. The right-of-way crew operating their forty-ton D-8 bulldozers pushed the giant trees over. The roots frequently did not break loose from the ground along the side where the tree fell. The sawmen cut the tree into logs, often allowing the stump to sit back upright and remain firmly attached to the earth.

Normally, I kept the boom as vertical as possible and raised the cable straight up from the log or stump, lifted it, and carried it away. When I couldn't break it loose, I started the cable and the boom going up at the same time. That worked until we confronted stumps that were even larger than those on higher ground. I then tried bringing the cable up with the boom, and running backwards simultaneously. That caused the tractor to stand on its nose. Frequently, the hooks would tear out and the tractor would come down with a tremendous jolt, causing the cable with the thirty-pound hooks to fly through the air. Sam ducked the hooks and invariably gave me a dirty look.

Eventually, we came to a stump we could not disengage. We wrestled around and around, pulled and pushed it until we were on the verge of being hopelessly bogged in the mud. I told Sam, "We've got to leave it."

He said, "Boss Red is going to raise more hell than a jilted widder when he sees a stump you've left in the right-a-way of his road." The next day we were forced to leave another stump.

The following morning, Boss Red passed me between the yard and the rough right-of-way, splashing mud in every direction. Sam said, "There he goes an' we ain't gonna have no more hair on our head than he's got, when he sees them stumps you left."

I asked, "What do you mean, you?"

He said, "I been knowing that man for thirty years an' when he gets up about something, it's ever' man for hisself."

Boss was waiting by the first stump. I cut the engine down to full idle. Boss Red said, "What the hell did I tell you to do here?" He spread his arms in a hopeless gesture indicating the huge stumps sitting in the right of way.

I was determined to stand up to him. I answered, "With all due respect, you gave me an order, but you didn't give me the tool to do it with." He climbed up on the machine and motioned for me to let him sit in the operator's seat. I jumped down while he moved the crane toward a stump.

Giving him credit for fairness, he tackled the biggest stump first. Sam hooked it and Boss Red began to do the same things I had done the day before to the same stump. He engaged the cable, raised the boom, and ran backwards at full speed. When the stump didn't move, the back motion brought the boom down, raising the rear of the tractor up in the back until it was almost vertical. The hook broke loose and the machine fell back, splashing mud in every direction.

The older man was not easily defeated. He tried wrapping the cable around the stump and hooking it to the back of the tractor and twisting it out. That didn't work. Sam said, "Boss Man, why can't I go get the men on the Big 8's back here? They can push 'em out."

Boss spit in the direction of the big tractors, "Because they have a job to do where they are, and besides, they are a mile ahead. That would cost two hours running time." He got back in his Jeep and spun around, heading back in the direction he had come. He yelled, "Come on, Sam, we are fixing to move some stumps." Sam caught him on the fly and they were soon out of sight. I went back to moving the logs and stumps that were not attached to the ground.

About eleven o'clock, I saw the old army jeep coming back, bucking and bouncing down the right-of-way. Sam was clutching a box of dynamite, trying to hold on and stay alive. They roared past me and stopped at the same stump Boss Red had wrestled with earlier. I couldn't hear what he was saying, but he was obviously directing Sam to place the dynamite under the stump, to punch out a hole with a steel bar in the soil directly beneath it, and to fill the hole with sticks of the volatile explosives.

It appeared Sam was too conservative with the dynamite. Boss waved him back and started stuffing the dynamite under the stump in a quantity that would demolish Stone Mountain. Lucille insisted I move back, then decided that I should move even further, while Boss Red added explosives. When he was satisfied, he uncoiled a fuse across the right-of-way and behind his Jeep.

I moved back a third time. Lucille said, "Not here."

I asked, "Where?"

She said, "Cross Creek."

Sam ran past me and into the woods, as if a pack of catch dogs was after him. I got off the tractor and crouched behind it.

The time passed slowly while the fuse burned. The swamp lay quiet. A thin wisp of blue smoke drifted from the woods beyond the stump. Then the earth exploded. The concussion jarred the swing crane and me, seeming to impact from all directions. The sky was obliterated with muck, mud, and pieces of stump.

A second of silence passed, followed by the whistling sound of falling debris. Fifty-pound fragments of the stump collided with the ground, making a sickening thud. Mud rained in droplets and lumps. Gradually, it subsided and stopped.

I peered over the tractor. I couldn't tell if Boss Red had fallen in the mud, or the mud had fallen on him. He was standing there covered in mud, and acting like he didn't know where he was.

The swamp lady came running out of the woods on the other side of the right-of-way, overweight, overwrought, and mean. She was wielding a battling stick, the kind used to beat dirt out of clothes after they are boiled in a 20-gallon iron wash pot. She headed straight toward Boss Red with her battling stick in the kill position.

Boss tried to keep the jeep between himself and his furious attacker, but she was not to be dissuaded. I couldn't hear what was being said, but it was clear Boss was trying to reason with her, and she wasn't buying it. Occasionally, she calmed for a few seconds, and then she would start waving the stick, threatening him again.

After ten minutes of serious negotiations, Boss came around the jeep and attempted to help her in. She pushed him away with her stick and climbed in. He ran around to the driver's side. She attempted to pin her dress in front with one hand, in order to contain her more-than-ample bosom, while keeping a firm grip on the battling stick with her other hand. Boss and his new acquaintance roared off in the direction of the highway.

Sam came out of the woods cautiously, looking up and then to one side, and then the other. He asked if anybody was hurt. I told him, "Nobody, yet."

He said, "I tried to tell Boss Red he got too many sticks under that stump, but Boss said he had never had to blow the same stump twice."

Two hours passed before we saw the jeep coming back. The swamp lady still held her stick on ready. A new cast iron wash pot sat like a trophy on the back of the Jeep. At that moment, Sam and I both realized what had happened—the concussion had busted the woman's wash pot, with her clothes boiling in it. We both grinned as they passed and got a look from Boss that would melt rocks.

A few minutes before quitting time, Boss Red emerged from the woods without the lady or the wash pot. He was almost casual as he walked over to where we were working. We said, "Good afternoon, Boss."

He ignored our greeting, "Did you fellows see anything unusual around here today?"

"No, sir," we both answered, sounding like we were a duet practicing for a funeral.

He said, "That's good. Because if you did, you might both be so far from here tomorrow, you would never find your way back."

We both repeated, "We didn't see nothin'."

He turned and got in his jeep and said without looking back, "I don't want to keep you men from your work, and, Sam, now you know how to blow the other stumps."

Before nightfall, everyone in that county knew every detail of how Big Red busted the woman's wash pot. But, no one laughed or said anything about it when he was around.

In July, we finished the road into the Apalachicola River. Then without missing a day's work, we moved to higher ground, building a road through the community of Two Egg in Jackson County. We continued to work ten hours a day, six days a week. Running the big machines was no longer exciting. In fact, it was boring. Up and down one section, and then moving up to the next.

I began to seriously think about what I wanted to do with my life. The list of things I didn't want to do had expanded from being in the livestock business, to the military, the grocery business, and throughout the summer, the road-building business moved up onto the list.

Finally, I thought I should reduce the problem to its most basic level. On the positive side, what did I like to do when pay and opportunity were not part of the consideration? That was simple: I liked to draw and paint. I liked art. I thought, "Why not? I have the GI Bill and a little money. I could go to an art school and become an artist." For the first time since I could remember, Lucille approved.

I told Clyde and his dad I wanted to leave the last week in August. Boss Red reckoned they would be able to build roads without me. The next two weeks didn't do anything to enhance my reputation. During that time, I turned a semi-tanker truck over, and busted the hydraulic system on the swing crane.

Lucille made a biggie out of the truck incident, and used it as final proof that I should separate myself from anything remotely associated with road construction.

I said goodbye to all my friends and boarded a Greyhound back to the Creek. Lucille sat up front with me.

Chapter 6

ART SCHOOL AND ROMANCE

When I arrived back at the Creek, Miz Rawlings was at her beach house in Crescent Beach, so I went to see my friend, Bernie Bass. Bernie was always like a dose of sunshine in a New England winter. He had experienced hard times and adversity most of his life, but remained undaunted. I told him I had decided to be an artist.

He smiled and said, "You can't beat that, J.T. Doin' what's important to you is better than being a big shot doing something you hate." He continued, "I knew a feller once up in Dixie County that wasn't good at nothing but being pore. The feller figured if he was gonna be pore anyway, he might as well be the poorest man in the county. That way, he would be somebody outstandin'. An' he was. 'Course, he had to work at it. Ever' now and then, somebody would give him somethin' to eat and the poor feller would have to eat it real quick so he could say he didn't have nothin' to eat. Sometimes, somebody would give him clothes, like a coat or new britches. He'd stomp on them, punch them full of holes, and then let the dogs sleep on them for a few days before he could be seen wearing them, all just to be the poorest man in the county and keep up his reputation. The feller served a good purpose in the community 'cause ever'body else could look down on him. The feller was happy to be outstandin' an' even a little bit famous."

After considering Bernie's philosophy, I told him I might try to be the worst artist in the country. He said, "That's shooting awful high." He slapped his knee, "I seen some pictures of New York art in a magazine that was worse than anybody could ever do without a lot of practice." I thanked him for his counseling, although I wasn't sure how I could use it.

Miz Rawlings came to the Creek for the weekend, so I went down to her house for a visit. She said she was mad at her birddog, Moe, because he had chewed up a bandanna in her car, coming back from Crescent Beach. I suggested it might be a bad time to visit, but she said it was a fine time. She missed the Creek when she was away. I told her I did too.

Miz Rawlings suggested we set on the back porch steps facing her garden.

We talked about her battle with the weeds and bugs for a few minutes, and then talked about my desire to study art. I told her everybody at the Creek thought it was a good idea except my Dad. She laughed loud and said she would not expect Tom Glisson to be enthusiastic for his son to become involved in the arts. I told her it created a quandary trying to figure what he wanted. He expected me to decide for myself what I should do, and then he usually disagreed, but he wouldn't like it if I gave in and agreed with him.

She laughed and said, "He is wiser than you think." She asked where I planned to go and if I needed help. I told her I had the GI Bill and had asked a professor at the University about schools. He had suggested The Art Institute in Chicago, The Art Students League in New York, or Ringling in Sarasota. I thought Ringling would be best for me. I liked being in Florida.

We sat for a few minutes and then in that articulate way she had of saying something she was positive about, she said, "J.T., you go to art school and I'll stay here and fight with your dad."

Lucille and I enrolled at Ringling and started classes in the fall semester of 1948. It was the most exciting and fulfilling thing I had ever done. The work of many of the first year students was better than I had hoped to do when I graduated. The professors said not to be discouraged, since most of the students had art education throughout high school, and some had excellent teachers in elementary classes. If I applied myself I would catch up by the end of the year.

Lucille loved Sarasota from the first day we arrived. It was a small Gulf Coast town with only 12,500 permanent residents. The town had a quiet, comfortable elegance inherited from the Palmers of Chicago and a reserved flamboyance contributed by the Ringling family. Like good wine, it had aged comfortably and acquired a special character of its own.

The crystal-clear, blue-green waters of the Gulf of Mexico, stretching along miles and miles of deserted white-sand beaches, made it a paradise even to a Cracker from the backwoods of North Central Florida.

Ringling School of Art's affiliation with the Ringling family gave students free access to the circus that wintered there. We frequently sketched and did watercolors on the circus grounds and became acquainted with most of the performers. The clowns were my favorites—Buzzy Pots, Lu Jacops, Emmett Kelly, along with several others. They were, in many ways, similar to the folks back at the Creek, friendly and comfortable.

Nearly all the trapeze performers had accents. Some had difficulty speaking any English, but they were hospitable and seemed as interested in my sketches as I was of their artistry. One of the acrobats asked what kind of accent I had, and I told him it was called Cracker, that the people where I came from also had trouble with the English language.

Cecil B. DeMille came to Sarasota to film the movie, *The Greatest Show On Earth,* while the circus was in its winter quarters. I was among the first extras hired to be in the cast of countless thousands for eighteen dollars a day and a box lunch. Dorothy Lamour, Gloria Graham, and Cornell Wilde were only some of the stars moving on and off the sets. The atmosphere was casual. They were not shielded as much as they would be today.

Charlton Heston sought out the art students during his breaks. I sat with him several times, and compared stories of his art school background and Ringling School of Art. My brief experience with the filming of *The Yearling* and the three weeks with DeMille's extravaganza hooked me on films and moviemaking. Besides, I liked saying, "I was in *The Greatest Show on Earth*."

Ringling's male students were mostly veterans enjoying a respite in a paradise they could not have dreamed possible during the war. They lived in a new dorm a hundred yards from the main building. The men had no curfews.

The girls were mostly straight out of high school. They lived in a dorm on the second floor of the main building. Studios, a lobby, an administrative office, and a large exhibit space occupied the first floor. The girls had a strict curfew, in at ten on weeknights and eleven on Saturdays. There were as many pretty girls in Sarasota as any place in America, but in Sarasota, skimpy bathing suits made them prettier.

My roommate was a tall, good-looking veteran from Birmingham. And I, like the girls in Lake Wales said, was a guy girls went with to prove that looks didn't matter. Until this day, I cannot recall how my roommate and I started stealing each other's dates. It became a game that we both worked at with enthusiasm during the first year. Bill would tell my dates that I was a cad and all kinds of things that were unfounded. When they were in shock, he would put on his "Southern Gentleman" manners and offer to fill in any vacancy he had created. Several times I no sooner met a girl than she would put her nose in the air like a horse that's afraid of the bridle, and stalk off without an explanation.

In that Lucille is looking over my shoulder, and the purpose of this narrative is to be contrite and repentant, it is only fair to admit that I was responsible for several of Bill's super dates taking flight and refusing to speak to him under any circumstance. All of which brings me to an episode that ultimately changed my life more than any other. Some called it a catastrophe, while Lucille thought it was sweet.

Shortly after Christmas, Bill woke me, moaning and clutching his side. He said he was suffering severe pain. I didn't have any penicillin or sulfa drug, which was what the army gave to anyone moaning, regardless of the symptoms. Because he was groaning so loud that no one could sleep, I borrowed a car and drove him to the hospital. They immediately removed his appendix.

I slept through the next morning because Bill had kept me up most of the night, and also because it was Saturday. In the afternoon, I met a friend of one of the girl students. She was the kind that would stand out at a beauty contest.

In fact, she had. She was a former Sarasota beauty queen, honey blond, with a figure that looked like it was designed by a consortium of Ferrari and Cartier. She told me she did charity work when she wasn't sailing.

I made a date with her on Sunday to go to the beach. Then I had a brilliant idea. I asked her if she would mind going by the hospital before going to the beach. I told her my roommate was there and I was concerned about his condition. She thought it was sweet of me to be concerned. I knew Bill was going to be confined to bed even after he got out of the hospital. He was helpless. I would show off my super date and then leave him with IVs and God-knows-what-else sticking in his body, while the catch-of-the-year and I went off to lie on a secluded beach.

Lucille had generally liked art school and confined her lectures to the risks of shark-infested waters and thunderstorms. She suddenly sprang into action, "You should be ashamed. It's not honest. He is your friend and she is innocent." I told her I thought she was supposed to be in charge of saving me from catastrophes, cataclysms, fiascos, and stuff like that. She said I was a fiasco, past, present, and future. I was undaunted.

With the jewel of Sarasota on my arm, I visited my sick roommate early the next afternoon. My date was luminous, exciting and charming. Bill was bug-eyed and mesmerized. I felt like Wellington after Waterloo and Henry Higgins after Julie Andrews finally "got it." I made small talk. I asked him if they had told him how much his bill would be and asked why his gown was so short. Then I told him we had to go since my date wanted to even her tan while there was plenty of sun.

The following day, I attended classes and worked in a studio until late afternoon, without going back to my room. About six, I combed my hair, tucked in my shirt, and walked to the former Sarasota beauty queen's home. I pushed the doorbell and almost simultaneously the door came open a few inches. My dream date's face was flushed and she literally spat her words in my direction. "You go and don't ever come near me again!" She slammed the door and yelled, "Daddy!" I, of course, retreated up the street bewildered for a few moments-that is, until I thought of Bill.

When I got back to the room, Bill was sitting up in his bed grinning like he had dined on canaries. I accused and he denied. I asked when and how he got out of the hospital. His doctor, Dr. Learn, who was aware that art students generally lived in the shadow of poverty, released him on the condition that he would stay in bed for a week, the only exception being to go to the bathroom. I knew he had gotten to the girl, but didn't know how. Bill said Doctor Learn was confident I would bring him his meals and see to his care. I told him to get ready to live on molded bread and stale water.

In spite of our shenanigans, we were friends and I hoped he would recover without complications. About eleven o'clock that night, Bill amazed me with the wildest request I could imagine. He wanted to visit his regular girl over in the girl's dorm. The only way that was possible was to climb up on an eight-foot- wide overhang that was suspended twelve feet above the sidewalk, and attached to the side of the girl's dorm. Male students frequently climbed up there and talked to the girls through the screens. It was against the school's rules, and on rare occasions the police would come by and turn their spotlight on anyone that was on the ledge. When that happened, the girls would open the screen and let the young man run through their room, across the hall to a fire escape on the opposite side of the building, hopefully before the house mother could get up and identify the culprit.

Bill said he wanted me to help him up. I told him he was insane, and pointed out that it had only been three days since they operated on him. He said, "It will surprise my girl."

I argued, "It'll surprise medical science if you survive." He said he was up to it, that all he needed was a boost up onto the roof. Bill had served in combat in the war and if he wanted to get on the roof he was going to. So I said, "O.K."

I boosted him up on a garbage bin and then up onto the roof. Since I would have to help him down, I climbed up and talked to some of the other girls while he visited his friend. Murphy's Law was activated and the police came around in a squad car. Naturally, they pointed their spotlight on us. I ran down to the opposite end, jumped off into the shrubbery and returned to the men's dorm. I assumed Bill would go through his girl's room as he had done before and out the fire exit.

I waited for a half hour before summoning a group of students who were three hours into a beer party. I told them I was afraid something had happened to Bill. They asked, "Why?" I explained the situation he was in, when I left him on the ledge.

With the subtlety of a Mardi Gras parade, they set out across campus to search for their former comrade-in-arms. I could not help but be reminded of a distinct similarity to the searches I had participated in back home, when my friend, Charley Fields, went on his annual drunk and was lost for three days. After more than a hour, we were about to give up, when one of the students reported he had found Bill lying in the shrubbery at the opposite end of the girls' dorm. Bill had jumped off the ledge at the same place I had jumped earlier. With a lot of unnecessary fanfare, the partying students carried him back to the men's dorm. Bill had broken open his incision and lost a little blood, but nothing alarming. We all agreed we had seen worse in the military. Nevertheless, it was necessary to call Doctor Learn.

The beer party continued in our room with everyone making jokes at Bill's expense, while he tried to come up with a plausible reason for his incision suddenly opening. Doctor Learn finally arrived looking like he had just got out of bed. He examined the incision and shook his head in amazement. "How did this happen? It was such a pretty incision."

Bill repeated the question, "How? I went to get a drink of water at the fountain and after that it opened up."

The compassionate Doctor continued to shake his head and said, "I have practiced medicine for nearly forty years and I have never had this happen."

Bill was the picture of innocence. I couldn't resist needling him. I asked, "Doctor, do you suppose the water fountain was too high?"

Bill said, "Glisson, don't you have something to do?" I suggested the Doctor take him back to the hospital. Bill told me to quit interrupting, and that he couldn't pay for more hospital time. The Doctor said he would have to put clamps on the incision and fill Bill with penicillin to keep it from getting infected. In addition, Bill would have to use a walker when he went to the bathroom for the next ten days.

With a pleading voice that was sincere, Bill asked if he could go to a Valentine dance on Saturday, not to dance, but only as an observer. I had asked the Sarasota beauty queen to attend that same dance, with me. The lights went on-the rascal had, in some way, sold me out and made a date to go with my super date. I said, "Doctor, I don't see how I can take care of him. He looks like he's in bad shape. What if I can't make him stay in bed?"

He replaced the kindly voice with a positively commanding one, "Bill, you will stay in the bed like I said. I don't want to hear any suggestions for anything different."

Bill said, "Yes, sir."

The doctor dressed the incision, and gave Bill a couple of shots. His agitation subsided. When he was ready to leave, he hesitated in the doorway, "Bill, you stay in the bed and when you are able to get around, I will introduce you to a very pretty nurse that recently joined the staff over at the hospital."

Bill asked, "Where's she from?"

Dr. Learn answered, "She is a graduate of Saint Vincent's in Jacksonville. I'll tell her tomorrow you are going to call. She needs to meet some young friends down here."

When the doctor was out of the building, I told my roommate, "You owe me and Sarasota's debutante-of-the-year a personal apology. If you expect to eat three times a day and listen to my radio for the next week and a half, you better call her and arrange a meeting for your official confession." He promised with his fingers crossed.

The next day, my old service buddy, Bob Hager, showed up on his annual winter holiday. He was driving a new, blood red, Ford convertible. He and the car couldn't have been more welcomed. We found him an extra bed in the dorm and he moved in. Hager sunned on the beach while I attended classes. When I was free, we cruised around or dated in the late afternoon and at night. Hager had joined the Air National Guard immediately after we were discharged and wanted me to join so we could meet and fly together on weekends. I told him I didn't want to be obligated to the military. He thought I was missing a great opportunity to have fun and see the country.

I will never know if it was Lucille or the devil that popped the thought into my mind, but as things turned out, I believe my guardian angel was feathering her nest. I was on my way to life class when an extraordinary thought suddenly occurred to me. "Why are we waiting for ol' Bill to get well? Why don't we call the new nurse at the hospital? After all, Dr. Learn said she needed friends in Sarasota. And I would be the perfect choice to fill in for the ailing Bill."

Lucille grumbled a little while I walked to the pay phone in the lobby, but not enough to dissuade me. I called the hospital and explained that Dr. Learn had mentioned a new nurse from Jacksonville in a social conversation and that he had suggested I give her a call. The operator hesitated and I added she is the one from Saint Vincent in Jacksonville. The operator said, "Oh, you must mean Miss Apone."

I said, "Yes, Miss Apone. Could you put her on?" Patricia Eileen Apone answered. I said, "I am the art student, one of Dr. Learn's friends. He suggested I call."

She said, "Oh yes, he spoke about you." I asked her if I could pick her up after work, that we could get a sandwich. She said, "That would be fine. I will be off duty at three." I liked her voice.

I cut the end of life class and Hager and I headed for the hospital. Before I went inside, I had an attack of acute apprehension. Suppose Dr. Learn was a poor judge of beauty. She might be mean as a snake or a shrew. There was one consolation—if I didn't like her, I could tell her I only came over to speak for my roommate, Bill. He wanted me to say hello and how much he was looking forward to meeting her when he was well.

Since I was a child at the Shriners Hospital in Greenville, I have been comfortable in hospitals and around nurses. These angels of mercy had a pure and reassuring quality in their white, starched uniforms. Certainly there is no profession that is nobler.

When I walked into the lobby of the old Sarasota Memorial Hospital and saw her coming down the hall, there was no doubt that she might be anyone other than the girl I had come to meet.

Lucille whispered, "Ahh, she is beautiful."

Birds sang and violets bloomed on the terrazzo floor. I knew that no matter what other wonderful events happened in my life, that moment would be one of the most precious, that instant when I met that lovely creature with the slender figure, the light brown hair and soft gentle blue eyes.

I forgot all the clever things I intended to say, walked her out to the car and introduced her to Hager, or maybe they introduced themselves.

We had a sandwich and Cokes at the local drive-in. She had tuna fish on toast and I had ham salad. Although her name was Patricia, she preferred to be called Pat. Her name could have been Berthalou and I would have loved it. Without any comprehension of what was happening, I had entered a world I didn't know existed.

Pat said she needed to get home and change from her uniform. I was terrified that she just wanted to get away politely. I tried to be as casual as possible and managed to ask her if she would like to go to the boat races on Sarasota Bay the next day. She said yes and suggested she might ask her sister, "Neen," to come along as a date for my friend. I said that would be great, before Hager had a chance to answer. With an inflection of total indifference he said, "That will be great."

We dropped Pat off on the south side, where she lived with her parents. Hager was afraid to go to the boat races. He said sure as glory my date's sister would be a dog. He complained, "Glisson, they are always the same. A good looker and one that ain't." He believed the sheet-metal sister he got in Lake Wales was a lucky draw. He pitched his voice higher. "Glisson, I do believe you are smitten. Next thing you will be telling me is you are in love." I ignored him and concentrated on keeping him from backing out on his date with Pat's sister.

The next day when we got to their house, Hager walked up the steps with the same reluctance he would have if there were thirteen steps with a rope swing at the top. Pat and her sister came out to meet us, and my buddy was instantly transformed into a beacon of shining gratitude. Neen was as cute as a pin with an infectious sense of humor that put every one at ease. The afternoon was magic. I told Pat some of the art students were cads and if any called her and tried to tell her they were supposed to call, she should hang up. Bill never said if he did and I never asked.

April in Sarasota comes in the late spring when the fragrance of orange blossoms and tropical flowers permeates the air. Pat, Hager and Neen watched the races while I watched Pat.

Lucille was strangely agreeable. She was not only understanding about how I fraudulently met my new girl, she actually implied there was no hurry to confess.

Hager stayed over a few days longer than he originally intended and left Sarasota planning to come back as soon as he could get a break. He told me, "Glisson, you are getting in deep with your girl, which is great if that is what you want." I disagreed. He said, "I have never seen you when your intentions were so honorable."

Neither of us knew that in a few short weeks our lives would change more than we could have believed possible. Hager's Air National Guard squadron was among the first called up in the Korean War. He distinguished himself flying P-51's and F-86's, earning the Bronze Star, Distinguished Flying Cross and a Purple Heart.

I dated Pat every time I had the opportunity, walking the five miles over to her home and then five miles back to the art school. I had a severe attack of shyness because I was afraid of losing her and stumbled over my shoelaces constantly.

The annual Beaux Arts Ball, held in the ballroom of the old John Ringling Hotel, was a favorite of the girls in Sarasota. If they dated an art student, they could go out to the circus' winter quarters and select any costume from the thousands Ringling Brothers had in their wardrobe. Some cost tens of thousands of dollars. I asked Pat and she accepted. I went as one of the four horsemen and she as a cheerleader.

On a Sunday, we went to the beach where I spent the afternoon trying to get up the nerve to kiss her. I fumbled around and never did. When I noticed the time, the lockers where we had our clothes were closed and the attendant had gone home. We got on a city bus in our bathing suits and begged fare from the passengers to get Pat and me back to her home. That evening, we listened to records because my money was locked up with my trousers at the beach.

About nine o'clock that evening, my brother called from the hospital in Gainesville. He said there had been an accident the doctors said that if I wanted to see my father before he died, I had better come immediately. Pat took me to the art school and she and the students loaned me enough money to rent an airplane to fly to Gainesville. A pilot friend volunteered to go with me and return the plane to Sarasota. We flew there in an old Cessna 140 with no landing lights and insufficient fuel to reach the nearest twenty-four-hour service facility in Tampa or Jacksonville. The chart said "lights on request in Gainesville."

When I arrived there, the airport was the darkest part of the city. I buzzed back and forth over the field, racing and cutting the throttle to attract attention, but no one switched the runway lights on. My fuel was going into the red so we crossed town to a dirt strip called Stingel Field. It was dark so I cut the throttle and raced the engine without a response. The last alternative was to attempt to land on a highway and risk the wires of both the telephone and power companies.

We were running on fumes when Lucille came through. A car pulled out from a beer joint across the road from the little airport and drove onto the field. Unfortunately, he parked at the wrong end, making it necessary to land downwind, shoot the landing in front of the car, and roll out in the dark. We touched down trying to remember where the strip was supposed to be. In the darkness, we passed between two parked planes that I would not have taxied between in the daytime, and rolled to a stop.

The Good Samaritan who heard our engine not only gave up his seat at the bar to drive out onto the field, he also drove me to the hospital.

My dad had mistakenly swallowed some poison he believed to be water and had no chance of surviving. We talked and he told me his philosophy of life being comparable to a trip on a train. It had a profound effect on me then and still does. His trip ended a few hours later.

I was devastated by my dad's death. Throughout his funeral and the days that followed, I felt a deep sense of loneliness mixed with a desire to be with Pat in Sarasota. It seemed selfish to think about my girl at a time when my family needed one another. I wished I had told him about her.

My sister-in-law asked me if I had a girlfriend. I answered, "Yes, her name is Pat and I am going to marry her." I was surprised more than my sister-in-law. It was the first time in my life I had thought of marriage. I had never even kissed my bride-to-be or told her I loved her. In fact, until that moment, I didn't know I was in love. It was like a great revelation that had suddenly come to light. Of course my sister-in-law told all the other women and they in turn told each other.

It should not have been a surprise that Lucille did cartwheels all over the place. She was obviously delighted with my emotional evolvement with the pretty nurse from Sarasota. In fact, only an idiot like me could have missed Lucille manipulating every little detail of the romance from the begining.

The only people who didn't know were the bride-to-be and my mother. I would attend to that as soon as possible and in that order. When the funeral and the administrative details were complete, I boarded the bus back to Sarasota. Lucille danced and pirouetted up and down the isles, making a nuisance of herself. She had a few little suggestions on what I should say to Pat. I told her to get lost, I intended to handle this circumstance by myself. She was undaunted as usual.

I tried to analyze the situation. Some facts were clear. Love with the opposite sex is quite different than love of family or a horse. It is a condition. Love is all consuming like the flu. Love affects the recipient's ambition, memory, priorities, and pocket book, not to mention his appetite, blood pressure and sleep habits. The condition in the advanced state exaggerates the victim's aggressive and wimpish characteristics. During the hippie era of the sixties, there was the Love Movement. Thankfully, it never got off the ground. If every one fell in love at the same time, the world would succumb to total chaos. Nothing would be on time; all institutions would collapse because of indifference.

I thought the first thing to do was to select just the right place for a romantic proposal, then to propose in elegant, chosen sophisticated words, and of course, I should bring flowers. I was still planning my proposal when the bus arrived in Sarasota shortly after dark.

I got off the bus and ran across town to Pat's house, went in on the porch and rang the doorbell. She came out. I grabbed her, kissed her, said, "I love you and will you marry me?"

She said, "Yes."

We set the date for September twentieth, five months from that day, two weeks before the beginning of the fall semester. I didn't learn a lot about art during the months that followed. Pat was assigned to a shift that started at three o'clock in the afternoon and worked until eleven o'clock each night. Every day after dinner, I walked across town to her house and waited for her to get off. I stayed until about two o'clock then walked back to the dorm. Many of the discrepancies in my art today are in areas that were taught in the eight-to-noon classes during that semester.

One evening, when I arrived at Pat's house, she was ecstatic. She said, "You won't believe what a wonderful surprise I have." I asked what it was and she said, "Because Dr. Learn introduced us and we were engaged to be married he has invited you and I to have dinner on his yacht."

I told her to sit down as Lucille was going out the door. I started out with, "I don't believe we should accept the invitation," and then said, "There is one thing I didn't tell you." I made a full confession and was undeservedly forgiven.

One other important matter had to be taken care of in preparation for our wedding day. Pat is Catholic, and told me I was supposed to go to the priest for the Church's instructions. I expected it to be heavy and was surprised when I arrived.

The old Monsignor had a chessboard set up and motioned me to sit across from him. He moved and I moved; he was devastating with his bishops. We played for an hour. He told me to come back the next day and I did. We played chess for two hours. He again told me to come back the next day and have Pat join us an hour later. I returned and we played chess.

When Pat came in, he instructed her to wait until we finished the game. When we finished, he said, "Now, about your getting married. You know the rules of the Church, but I have two things I want you to promise me before I will bless your marriage. First, promise you will not try to impose your religious beliefs upon one another." Then he got a twinkle in his eye that was more Irish than it was Catholic. "Secondly, I want you to both promise me that after you are married, you will never exaggerate when you argue." I have always believed that the second promise was inspired by Lucille.

When school closed for the summer, I went up to Cross Creek to wait for the grand occasion.

Chapter 7

A SUMMER WITH MOMMA

Life at the Creek was always changing but it felt good to be back. I stayed with my mother and slept in my old room. Home was different. My dad was gone and the house and yard seemed to have taken on a nuance that was uncommonly special.

Like most kids, I had always taken the house and yard, and even the grove, for granted. Now, as an adult, I walked through the house, room to room. Everything was in its place, but more personal than I had remembered. I noted Momma's old pedal Singer sewing machine the one she had made and patched the family's clothes. The fireplace, where I had sat on the floor by the wood box and listened to my parents' conversations about their youth and family history, took on new significance.

There were the new additions that came from the fruits of my parents' labor, such as the bathroom with the only eight-foot bathtub I had ever seen. (My dad had said he wanted one he could stretch out in.) The window-seat with a space beneath it where my mother had stored her Christmas fruitcakes as far back as I could remember. She made them in October and seasoned them with whiskey until the holidays.

Every room held objects, changes, and even scratches that were like a diary of my family. There was a plug in the floor where the icebox drained before we got a refrigerator. In the back of my mind, I knew I was about to separate myself from this place, this home. I would always be welcome here, but to quote my dad, "Men marry off, not on."

The humanity of my mother began to become a reality. I recognized that she was the one who had taught me thousands of essentials to life itself, shoe-tying, table manners, cleanliness, the necessity for clean socks and underwear. Shamefully, I had been a reluctant student. Although I should not have been, I was surprised when she told me she had been terribly lonely after my dad died. Until then, I never knew that my mother could be lonely.

"Life goes on," she told me and it certainly had with her. She had converted my dad's cattle from Brahmas to the more gentle Black Angus. The citrus was in great shape, the grove clean of weeds, and the trees green and healthy. She had bought a piano and spent hours playing it in the glassed-in sun porch on the back of the house. She laughed, "Only me and the dog like my music and he doesn't have a choice."

Life was different, but the ambience of the Creek was still there. I don't remember a quieter, more peaceful summer.

I visited my friend, Bernie, and told him of my pending marriage. I confided in him that there were questions about weddings I could not answer. He laughed and said he had the same problem. "Why does the man have to go in the back door of the church and wait there until the bride gets good and ready for the wedding to start?" he asked. "And why does everybody have to stand up like the county judge is coming, before the bride comes in the front door and sashays up the isle?"

I added a question while he laughed. "Why does the girl's father give her away but nobody gives the groom away?"

Bernie said, "That's because the gal's daddy wants to be sure he won't have to finance another wedding." He wondered why they call the man who is not getting married the "best man." I told him the women said it was tradition. He said that brought up another question. "Why is everything tradition when they are doing it the first time?" Bernie said the smartest man in the world was probably Bernard Baruch, and he bet Bernard didn't understand weddings either. I told him if Mr. Baruch ever comes to visit Miz Rawlings here at the Creek, we should ask him.

When I left home to go in the army, I was trying to make the transition from teenager to adult. (Some would say I never made it.) After being discharged, I was occupied with the grocery business and road construction. Then college and girls. I spent very little time at home. For the first time in my life, Momma and I were the only ones there.

During the days, we puttered with the things she wanted done around the house. In the evenings, we sat on the porch and talked until past midnight. I came to know my mother as a person and was pleasantly surprised with whom she really was. She told me of her childhood dreams; of studying social graces, and dresses that she thought were magnificently beautiful. And she admitted skipping school on one occasion. She told me of teenage infatuations with local boys and the subtlety of courtship when she was a girl.

In the evenings, I pulled my bed up along side the windowsill and put the pillow against the screen the same way I had kept it when I was growing up. I liked to lay with my head in the moonlight or staring up into the star-filled universe. Luxury doesn't have to cost anything.

I spent hours sorting out the woman who had been my mother for more than two decades versus the one I was getting to know. The affiliation of a child with one's parents and relatives, as well as the mystical relationship with a guardian angel, was baffling at best. My momma was tender, loving, and firm. My guardian angel was always persistent, and unyielding. That didn't leave me a lot of room for self-determination.

Life at the Creek was always changing, but it felt good to be back.

One likes to think his mother was the best mother in the world. Quite naturally, I believed mine was. While I was still a teenager, it became apparent to me that my mother was not your average mother; she was a product of her background.

Momma was born on a large farm in southwest Georgia. She had five older sisters and three younger brothers. Pearlee Josey came out of the cradle determined not to be ignored, nor to be second. They tell me she was witty and vivacious as a child, and pretty and independent as a teenager. She learned to keep the books for the farm, and earned her father's favor. However, an incident that occurred in her sixteenth year temporarily dampened Charley Josey's regard for his daughter.

My dad had told me about it in strict confidence. "The year before your momma finished high school, her dad enrolled her in a private college only a few miles from where they lived." While preparing for school, she embarked on what became to be known as Pearlee's ox fiasco. Dad laughed, "You know how she is when she sets her mind on something. When I heard about it, I wanted to meet her." He told me his version of the story.

"Your momma had heard stories of the power and virtue of oxen from her grandparents. She apparently pictured herself using a pet ox to pull her buggy onto and from campus' like a student today would be proud of an antique car to sport around in." My dad said Momma casually mentioned the breaking of an ox to her father. Her dad's reaction indicated he thought it was a dumb idea and certainly not a proper thing for a young lady to attempt. She was determined, but thought it best not to pursue it further with her father. After much persuasion, bribery, and threats, her younger brother slipped one of her father's young steers into a backfield. The two spent every minute of their free time, plus a tremendous number of hours stolen from other family duties, taming and breaking their charge.

Unfortunately, the ox, which Pearlee had named Rose Bud, had no intention of becoming anyone's beast of burden. But Pearlee's determination eventually prevailed. Rose Bud finally accepted the harness and learned to obey her commands.

Momma's brother said, "We still won't know if we've got us a real ox until we hitch him to a cart." Pearlee's dad didn't have any carts, and the Josey farm wagons were all designed for two horses. But there was one vehicle that would be perfect, Charley Josey's new, thousand-dollar, one-horse buggy, finished in black lacquer and gunmetal pin stripes. Her brother said "No! Absolutely not! Never!" But again, Pearlee prevailed and she and her brother bided their time until their father went on an overnight trip to a cotton gin in Iron City.

The ox performed splendidly. With Pearlee holding the reins and her brother bemoaning their fate if something went wrong, they drove Rose Bud down a seldom-used road through the piney woods avoiding any neighbor seeing their inaugural run in the event it was not a success.

The months of ox breaking seemed worthwhile until the unexpected happened. Without warning, Rose Bud crumpled to the ground, rolled his eyes back in his head, and for all purposes, appeared dead.

Pearlee screamed, "Dear Lord! He's had a heart attack! We have killed him."

Her brother was disgusted and threw his cap on the ground. "No, he ain't dead. He's sulled. That is what he has done. He's sulled."

Pearlee jumped from the buggy wringing her hands, saying, "Let's don't panic."

Her brother continued, "I have been told, with good authority, once an ox sulks, he will do it any time he pleases from then on. Sulking is what an ox or cow does when it gets tired of doing something it didn't want to do in the first place."

That did it! Pearlee spoke directly to the ox, "This Josey girl is not only as stubborn as you, she is a woman of action. So now, Mr. Rose Bud you lay there and watch me!" Using her fingers, she raked the dry pine needles that covered the ground around the sulking beast and piled the straw over the ox until only his head was visible.

Her brother watched, not knowing what his sister intended to do. Talking to himself he continued, "There ain't nothing gonna cause that ox to move. We've got to unhitch him and go off and leave him alone. He'll get up when he's good and ready and go back to the house. The best thing we can do is go get a horse to pull Pa's buggy home."

Pearlee gave no sign of hearing what he had to say. She planted her feet, wiped her long hair back from her face and said, "You just watch me! We'll see who continues to sulk." Rose Bud lay with his eyes rolled back, pretending to be dead.

With one hand holding the reins, Pearlee set the straw on fire. White smoke billowed.

Rose Bud knew when he was licked. Preserving as much dignity as possible, he slowly got to his feet and walked forward until Charley Josey's thousand-dollar buggy was directly over the fire. Then he balked again. Pearlee and her brother managed to unhook the ox, but the new buggy with its black lacquer finish and canvas top was totally destroyed.

Everyone in Decatur County had a good laugh, except Pearlee and her father. Since then her determination has been legendary.

My dad suggested, "I wouldn't mention anything about your momma's ox if I were you, son, I made the mistake of teasing her about it while we were engaged and she damn near refused to marry me."

That summer, while spending time with Momma, letters came regularly from Pat and my friends in Sarasota. They praised me for being so helpful with the wedding. Consequently, I idled my time while they planned and implemented it. Lucille seemed to have disappeared, causing me to suspect she had stayed in Sarasota to direct as much of the wedding plans as possible.

My mother was not so subtle, she admonished me. "Weddings are for the bride. Do what you are told to do and stay out of the way."

All this was in contrast with the determined woman I thought I knew. Typically, no one knew Momma had embarked on a campaign until she had a full-scale crusade under way.

For example, I remembered Momma announcing casually, "It's a pity that a family living in the country does not have a decent place for a few chickens to provide young, tender fried morsels for the family table; not to mention fresh eggs that have not set in a store for weeks."

My dad was not only smarter and wiser than I am, he had over a quarter century of experience to anticipate the motivation prompting Mama's announcements. He would finish his breakfast rather suddenly, pick up his hat and say, "I have to see a man about a horse. I will be back in time for supper." Going out the door he would look back over his shoulder and say, "J.T., you help your momma with whatever she needs done today." He was gone before Momma had time to protest.

Nevertheless, she would say to the door, "Tom, you know J.T. is the poorest help anywhere." I realized that I had just been committed to another of my mom's enterprises.

The rural mailman came through the Creek about nine thirty. The dawning of reality hit me when Momma just happened to be on the front porch when the mailman stopped at our box. She would brush me aside and greet Mr. Baker with a cheery good morning. He would smile and say, "I believe I have a package for you today, Mrs. Glisson." Through the window, he would pass a cardboard box with little half-inch holes cut around the entire perimeter. There was a peep, peep, peep sound coming from the box; in fact, dozens of peep, peep, peeps.

Since I could remember, my dad had said he didn't think it was practical or profitable to raise chickens, especially in light of my momma's compassion for little things like biddies and big things like milk cows. According to her, it was sorry and shameful not to feed the best quality and largest quantity of food attainable to anything the Lord had placed in your care. In fact she would quote a part of some verse that closed any rebuttal to her particular point. I was twenty years old before I realized that some of Mama's *Bible* verses were never printed. Dad had refused to build a chicken house for twenty-five years. Nevertheless, Mama ordered fifty biddies from Sears Roebuck every spring for twenty-five years, and improvised their housing facility.

Before I was nine or ten, my reputation for reliability was shot with Momma and Lucille when it came to chickens. One of the first tasks assigned to kids in the country was gathering eggs. It most certainly was not like an Easter egg hunt. We had orange crates with Spanish moss padding for nests, which were set up in orange trees for the hens to deposit their eggs.

I particularly hated the nests that were placed higher than my head. Frequently, when I reached up to probe in the nest, a hen would fly out, startling me into a state of paralyzed terror. The thing I dreaded most was when a big chicken snake came slithering out across my hand. I developed a habit of forgetting the high nests. Momma would complain that the hens were not laying as much as she expected. I chose not to confess. Then occasionally, I suspect with Lucille prompting, Momma would decide to gather the eggs and discover seven or eight in one nest, and a dozen in another, all spoiled.

When the nights were too cool, she would say, "The poor little things are out there shivering and it will hardly be any trouble to light a kerosene lamp in that crate to keep the little helpless things warm."

My dad would say, "J.T., help your momma."

Two weeks later, the pens I had just "helped" build were too small. She never said the chickens were getting too big. She said the crates were too small. So my dad had to see a man about a horse again, until Momma finished supervising the building of a bigger pen.

It is amazing how fast chickens grow, when for every three inches they grow taller, you have to build a bigger pen. The pens were so temporary they soon fell down and the whole process had to be done again the next year. She justified her chicken projects with, "I don't hear any complaints when you sit down to a plate of fresh tender fried chicken." That point was well taken.

It was a mystery how my dad could predict when Momma was going to have a sudden compulsion to grow things like chickens or vegetable gardens; not to mention a simultaneous passion to sun the mattresses and wash everything in the house.

Just before I left to go into the service, I asked him, "How do you know beforehand when Momma is going on one of her planting and cleaning spells?"

He said, "Son, it's just in all women's nature. All women go to nesting in the spring. There is nothing on heaven or earth that will deter them. But if a man can stay out of the way, it always passes in a few weeks."

After my father passed away, Momma met her Waterloo. When my brother came back from the Canal Zone, he brought with him two creatures, a monkey named Screwdriver and a parrot we later referred to as Potluck. Momma announced she didn't want anything to do with either of the foreign critters. My sister and I were surprised when she allowed the aliens on the place. We decided she was getting older and mellower. That was a miscalculation.

The new odd couple at the Glisson house settled in. With only a few minor skirmishes, they seemed at home. The parrot quickly learned to imitate everyone's voices. When he imitated Momma, it irritated her and she would tell him to hush. The parrot in turn would tell her to hush and she would throw a blanket over the cage. The parrot went too far when one of the ladies of the home demonstration club came and the parrot imitated her with some of the latest gossip. Potluck disappeared shortly after that. Momma would not discuss his sudden departure, but her grand kids teased that they were scared to eat chicken at Grandma's.

Screwdriver's tenure ended even more suddenly. During nesting season as my dad called it, Momma got Aunt Martha and one of her daughters to help wash all the blankets and quilts. This was a major job, which took seven hours. When finished, Momma sat eating her lunch, and heard her boxer dog and the monkey frisking around out back. She got up to see what they were doing. Screwdriver was running up and down the clotheslines, pulling out the clothespins, dropping the quilts into the dirt; and the dog was dragging them out into the orange grove through sandspurs and weeds. When momma ran out, the dog escaped, but the monkey was not so quick.

Momma caught Screwdriver by the leash. At that moment, a lady came around the corner of the house and exclaimed, "Oh, I see you have a monkey! I have always wanted one."

Momma mumbled one of her profusion of *Bible* quotes. "The Lord works in mysterious ways." She said, "Lady, you have a monkey now!" She shoved Screwdriver into the woman's arms and said, "Now take him and leave. I have a lot of work to do." The bewildered lady stood there for a few moments, then put the monkey in her car and left.

My mother was generally more polite. However, the lady had picked a bad time for a visit. It had been a really wonderful summer. I had enjoyed living at home that last time, hearing Momma's stories, and learning to know and understand her and my self. My residence had ended in the Glisson house along with my beloved Cross Creek. My bachelor status was also abruptly about to end.

Lucille reappeared at the Creek and escorted me to Sarasota for the big event.

Chapter 8

MISS APONE MARRIES LUCILLE AND ME

I arrived back in Sarasota ready to get on with the wedding and live happy ever after.

Ignorance is bliss, especially when it pertains to men and weddings. In 1950, at the ripe old age of twenty-three, I was loaded with ignorance and consequently lived in a state of bliss. When I was half that age, I thought getting married was something people did at the courthouse on Saturday afternoons when it didn't interfere with more important things.

I was present at only one church wedding before mine. I was then pushing twelve years old. The preacher announced there would be a wedding following the morning service. My feelings were anything but sentimental appreciation for the opportunity to attend a wedding. My only thought was this would delay Sunday dinner.

The couple wore their Sunday clothes, and the bride put a piece of what I thought was white mosquito netting over her head so that it covered her face. My sister said it was a veil. The man's shirt collar was too tight and his coat was too big. His face was pale like he had the flu.

Momma squeezed me against the pew, and whispered, "Don't laugh. Don't even smile." Even though that happened before I knew Lucille was around, I am sure she would have been even more righteous about weddings than Momma. All the men seemed uncomfortable and squirmed and pulled at their collars throughout the ceremony. I decided they were hungry, like me, and wanted to get home to their dinners. Some of the women cried when it was over. I asked why.

Dad said, "Son, if you every find out why, you tell me."

When Pat and I were going together, I would ask her what she wanted to do and she would invariably answer, "Whatever you want." She consulted me on even the most frivolous matters. She asked things like should she wear the red or the pink belt. I, of course, was glad to share my wisdom with her and to be honest, it made me feel taller. That all changed when it came to planning a wedding, and until this day no one has told me why.

Lucille was certainly no help. I considered it her primary function to rescue me in situations that were beyond mortal control. She insisted on extending her power base into what she called a catastrophe-prevention role. She harped on risky decisions and the necessity of avoiding escapades that defied the laws of physics. I thought she was becoming a busybody. She said, "I heard that."

My decision to get married and my choice of a bride was the first thing I could remember Lucille enthusiastically approving. She was so excited she was giddy, popping around and even pampering me. Somewhere in the recesses of my mind, it occurred to me that my decisions might be more Lucille's than mine. It occurred to me that she might extend her enthusiasm too far. I told her she was not going on the honeymoon. Pat and I were going alone. She acted hurt. I repeated, "Not on this honeymoon."

She responded, "I don't know why married men think they don't need angels." She hummed for a few seconds and said, "Some day you may yell for me and I may not answer."

The wedding was uneventful after I got my nosebleed stopped. The blood was not the result of the wedding, or at least not directly. The day of the wedding, I was dressing as carefully as possible, with Lucille looking over my shoulder and being officious as usual. She spotted a single hair up in the cavity of my nose and said it had to go. I took my safety razor and tried to get it in position to clip the little rascal. The task required determination, but after some contortions that could have gotten me in a sideshow, I accomplished the job. The problem came when I was attempting to remove the razor and made a substantial incision inside the nostril. I yelled at Lucille to stop the blood. She told me to calm down, that losing my temper would only make it bleed more. I told her I thought it was her job to save me from calamities and not to create them. I drove to the church with an ice bag on my nose.

Pat and I were married at four p.m., September 20, 1950. Pat's sister was the maid of honor and Lucille was an indiscernible bridesmaid. My best friend, Bob Hager, was in Korea so I enlisted the only art student that had a suit as my best man. I don't remember his name. Pat wore a light blue taffeta dress and a little pillbox hat with a short veil. She was beautiful. The ceremony proceeded without a hitch. However, even though Lucille had finally gotten the nosebleed stopped, I was afraid to say, "I do," above a whisper.

The reception was at Pat's home on Wood Street. There, she changed into a cantaloupe-colored, open-shoulder cotton dress. While we ate her father's cake and drank his champagne, one of the art students casually asked, "Which car are you going to use on your honeymoon?"

I thought, "I might be ignorant about weddings, but I know about decorating a honeymoon vehicle." I pointed to my mother's new Cadillac parked in front of the car I had borrowed for the trip.

When Pat was ready, we said goodbye, then ran out past my mother's overdecorated car and got into the sedan my sister had loaned me. The last we saw of my student friends, they were desperately stripping the decorations off my momma's car under her strict supervision..

The trip was uneventful except for being stopped in Naples by a Florida Highway Patrolman. The patrolman, at the request of one of my dear friends from the wedding party, acted as if he believed I had stolen my sister's car. After the joke was over, he wished us a long and happy marriage.

My wife and I drove across the Tamiami Trail to Miami and then on to Miami Beach where we checked into the Tides Hotel in the area that is known today as the Art Deco district. At 2:00 a.m., the sleepy desk clerk didn't care whether we were newlyweds or if we were there for our golden wedding anniversary. We shared a smug feeling of accomplishment at checking in unobtrusively without being identified as newlyweds. That lasted until we came out of the elevator the next morning. All the ladies in the lobby stared over and under their glasses and gave Pat a tight-lipped knowing smile. It was my first encounter with a predominantly Jewish group of women, and the first thing I learned about these wonderful people is, there is nothing Jewish women love more than a bride, and nothing less important than a groom.

Miami was an exciting place in 1950. It emerged from its role as a W.W. II Air Corps training center to become the place to go and be seen among winter tourists. Airlines were becoming a serious threat to the railroads, making it possible to fly there from the northeast in six or seven hours. Pan American Airways expanded service to and from South and Central America, introducing an additional market from the south. Low cost flights to and from Cuba made Havana a suburb of Miami.

Pat and I spent the days going about the city mesmerized by the lush tropical foliage, especially the poincianas that formed a flaming red canopy over many of the streets. We marveled at the crimson petals that had shed to the pavement, creating a red carpet suitable for a royal procession.

Our last day in Miami, we explored Coral Gables which was a product of the Florida boom. We drove down the wide avenues, past gateways and fountains that had graciously aged, peering at the soft yellow Spanish-style homes roofed with terra cotta tiles. The Gables was designed to be the most beautiful city in the world and was worthy of the title back then.

In the late afternoon, we drove through Coconut Grove and past the deserted John Deering Estate. Then while the last radiance of a majestic sunset faded over Miami, we came upon a new bridge leading off South Biscayne Boulevard and crossing what was obviously Biscayne Bay. The bridge appeared complete, only a single barrier with a red lantern blocked a small portion of the right of way.

There is something about bridges that challenge me to cross over to the other side and though I have no business there, I am compelled to cross. I told Pat we would drive out far enough to get a view of the Miami skyline. She questioned whether we should. It seemed a perfect opportunity for an innocent adventure, and there was an added incentive in that Lucille was back in Sarasota and would not be available to disapprove from the back seat.

We drove past the little barrier and out onto the snow-white, four-lane bridge. A cool breeze initiating from the Gulf Stream intermingled with the pink glow of a sunset reflecting up from the Gulf of Mexico a hundred miles to the west. We thought that the sky looked as if Paul Gauguin's palette had been used to create a theatrical backdrop for Miami's infant skyline.

We drove four or five miles until we reached the east end of the bridge where we stopped, got out, and watched the western sky. It turned deep red, then slowly transformed into the violet of bougainvilleas, and finally dissolved into the softness of a tropical night.

Pat and I stood there enjoying the soft breeze that smelled of saltwater blended with a thousand tropical flowers, until we became aware that our bodies were casting shadows from the moon rising behind us.

We turned and surveyed the area leading onto the island. Several pieces of construction equipment were parked just off the bridge, probably waiting for transport to another site. The sand and shell road leading onto the island was not paved but looked solid. I couldn't resist venturing further. I asked Pat if she would like to drive onto the island, just to see what it was like. She nodded yes.

Past a narrow strip of mangrove, we were surprised to find ourselves in a coconut plantation. The magnificent palms had been planted in rows, and they now curled fifty feet from the sandy soil. They were illuminated by a three-quarter moon, which had transformed twilight into moonlight with such subtlety that only the wild things were aware of the change. A sand road ran south, down the center of the island, paralleling the Atlantic Ocean, which was only fifty yards to the east, glittering in the moonlight. We drove without lights, listening to the hushed sound of ground swells colliding with the beach, mixed with the rustle of palm fronds overhead. I followed the road more than three miles, cruising along in second gear until we came to a spot open to the ocean.

It was one of those moments of perfection we like to think are exclusively ours: the perfect place at the perfect time and with the person whom one would most like to share it. My bride and I were lovers lost in paradise, unequaled and unexpected. I turned off the switch and pulled Pat closer, just as several thousand ravenous saltwater mosquitoes attacked, stinging all of our exposed skin through the thin tropical garments we were wearing. Pat screeched, "This is terrible! Get me out of here! Please hurry!"

I turned the switch to start the engine. It responded with a weak "uuh-uh" and then nothing. I looked at the instrument panel. The gas gauge was sitting below empty. We were out of gas on an island several miles from a gas station, with the meanest killer mosquitoes I had ever encountered.

We rolled up the windows, only to trap more of them than we could ever kill. I yelled for Lucille and slapped mosquitoes, then tried to brush them off Pat's back where she could not reach. I tried to assess our situation. With the windows up, it was too hot to stay in the car. The mosquitoes back at Cross Creek were not bad as long as a person walked at a fast pace, especially if one walked into the wind. I didn't know how far Pat could go in her medium height heels, and to add to the confusion, Lucille was suddenly there yelling, "Get out of the car!"

"Where did you come from?" I asked.

Her answer was, "Get out of the car."

I asked my wife of five days if she thought she could walk back to the mainland. She said, "Is there an alternative?"

Once we were out of the car and moving, the situation improved, but not to the extent it could be tolerated for any length of time. A few feet from the car, I caught a glimpse of a single weak light farther down the island. I don't know what we expected to find, but both of us were drawn to it like proverbial moths to a flame, even though it was a quarter-mile farther from the bridge and the security of the city.

Fifty yards from the light, we became aware the weak bulb was situated on a post extending up from a wall, ten or more feet from the ground. Portions of the structure that were visible above the overgrown shrubs and wall revealed an old two-story Spanish-style structure similar to the homes in Coral Gables. Coconut palms trailed moving shadows along the faded pink compound and its weathered terra-cotta roof. In any other circumstance, the place would have been a romantic creation worthy of a great love story or a Humphrey Bogart-type mystery.

Our situation was anything but romantic. I called, "Hello!" The sound seemed to die a few feet from where we were standing.

Pat called, "Hello! Will somebody please answer?"

I called again and waited. For all I knew the place might have been deserted before Pat and I were born. I didn't have the heart to tell her my thoughts, so I called again.

We waited, experiencing multiple panic and anxiety attacks, when a silky voice that sounded like a six-year-old's said, "Yessss." We both jumped back. A lady was peering over the wall to our left, in a direct line between the moon and us. Her long silver-gray hair glowed in the moonlight, exaggerating her silhouette to look like a siren in a Maxfield Parrish illustration. We were so startled we didn't answer until she spoke again. "Can I help you?"

Pat pleaded, "Oh yes, please do." Then in a stream of words and tears hidden by the shadow of the wall, she blurted out our dilemma.

"We're on our honeymoon, and we drove onto this island, and it was the most beautiful place I have ever seen. Then we stopped and the mosquitoes were eating us alive, and we were out of gas and we had to go for help, and we saw your light and we need help. Can you please help us?"

The lady in the moonlight answered in a soft compassionate voice that had an undertone of inbred refinement. "I have no gas, but perhaps you could accompany me back to the other end of the island. I think we might get some there."

I said, "That would be wonderful if you could."

Pat reiterated, "Wonderful, wonderful."

The lady disappeared for a moment, then suddenly emerged through a wrought-iron gate in the wall. She was wearing a wispy mid-calf-length nightgown that was white, or possibly a pastel. The exact color was indiscernible in the moonlight. Her hair looked as if it was generally unruly and had been let down and brushed before retiring. She led us around to the other side of the compound to a vehicle covered with a tarpaulin. I helped her remove the tarp and was surprised to see a contraption that could no longer be called a car, with no body, no fenders, and no seats. It was less than what we call a beach buggy.

Our rescuer said, "I hope it will start." She climbed up onto the bench behind the steering wheel, and Pat and I scrambled up on the passenger side. Without any tone of apology, she said, "It doesn't have any lights. There is no need on the island." The engine started and was unexpectedly quiet. If it didn't have anything else, it had a good muffler and exhaust system. We cruised back up the island, in and out of the shadows of the coconut palms, the lady's hair blowing in the wind.

What had been a horrible situation a few minutes before seemed an almost festive one now.

Pat said, "This is magnificent. Cruising on a tropical island in the moonlight with no lights or traffic." I agreed.

Our chauffeur and rescuer laughed. "I must confess; I often drive on the island in the moonlight."

We came to the area where the bridge builder's equipment was parked. There was also a large portable fuel tank. The lady stopped, retrieved a tin can from beneath her vehicle bench, and lifted the hose that led from a small hand pump, which was attached to the top of the tank. She hesitated for a moment, sniffed the end of the hose and said, "Good. It's gasoline." She filled the can, wedged it back under the seat, and we were off. I wondered if she knew the people who owned the equipment and the gas, but decided not to question the source of such philanthropy.

The jaunt back down the island was even more exhilarating. When we arrived at our car, she pulled up along side and waited with the motor running, until I poured the contents of the can into our car and returned the can to its place beneath the bench. I wanted to compensate her or at least thank her. Pat

and I both began at the same time, but were interrupted by a waving gesture of her hand that clearly indicated silence. "I hope you a long and happy marriage," she said, and drove away.

I started the car before the mosquitoes organized another assault, and we were off. We drove back up the island, across the new bridge, and back to the modern comfort of the Miami Beach hotel, without speaking. The reality or lack of reality, the seclusion, and the primitive beauty were all overwhelming, and could only be digested with the passage of time.

Lucille accompanied us throughout the rest of our honeymoon. She obviously did not trust me off on my own.

The following year, I finished art school, and the three of us moved to Miami where I could find employment in an advertising agency. Before unpacking the car, we drove back over the bridge identified with official road markers "Rickenbacker Causeway." We drove onto Biscayne Key, which had been elevated to a more fashionable Key Biscayne. The trail Pat and I had followed in the moonlight was paved with signs identifying it as Crandon Boulevard. A parking lot ran parallel to a public beach, which was filled with families cavorting in the sand and surf.

Like my home at Cross Creek, it had changed. It was still beautiful, but different. Some development had begun further down the island among the coconut palms, but we could not find the pink house we had been led to in the moonlight.

Pat immediately found a job at the new Mercy Hospital, which had been built on a part of the old John Deering Estate. But finding work for an inexperienced commercial artist was not so easy.

After several unsuccessful inquiries, I cut the advertising agency listings from the yellow pages of our phone book. Every morning, with Lucille tagging along, and with the list in my hand, I went from one agency to another, following the order in which they were listed. I asked for a job, and they all said they didn't have an opening or they were looking for someone with more experience. There were only nine agencies and art services in the Miami area, so I made the round every three days. After a couple of weeks, the receptionists became amused or, frequently, annoyed.

One morning, I went into the Newman Lynde Agency in the old Congress Building in downtown Miami. The receptionist looked up and said, "Mr. Glisson, you have been here several times before and each time you were told there was no opening. There is no opening and no reason for you to keep coming here." I pulled out the Yellow Pages listing and pointed out the agency listing.

She said, "So?"

I said, "You are on the list, and the list has the only places that employ artists. So, I have to keep coming until one of the places on this list hires me."

She waved her arms in frustration. "You are wasting my time and your time."

I think Lucille prompted me. I told the receptionist, "If you will let me talk to the art director, I will take your name off the list for a week."

She said, "That is impossible. He is a very busy man. He is having to get ahead with his work because he goes turkey hunting the first week of turkey season and that begins next week."

This was something I was familiar with. I told her, "If you will tell me where he turkey hunts, I will see him there."

A deep booming voice came from one of the rooms off the reception room. "Did I hear someone say something about turkeys?" Russ Smiley, six-foot-three, strong and naturally friendly, came out and shook my hand. "Are you a turkey hunter? Where are you from and where do you hunt?" I managed to say Cross Creek before he could interrupt. Russ said, "This is no place to talk turkey hunting! Let's go to lunch where we can really talk turkey!" On the way out the door, he told the receptionist, "Call Bob Eslinger and have him meet us. He's a turkey hunter and will want to meet this fellow."

I didn't eat much of my lunch because I was busy answering questions and listening to stories about turkey hunting in the Everglades. Nothing was said about art and agency jobs. Finally, Russ looked at his watch and said, "Damn! I have to get back to the office." He got up, grabbed the check and said, "Come on, Glisson. We have to give you a job. We're not going to let another turkey hunter get out of Miami." I had my first job as a commercial artist, without anyone asking where I studied or even looking at my portfolio.

My boss and art director, Russell Smiley, was born only a few yards north of the mouth of the Miami River. Russ was a wildlife artist and hunter. He had explored all of Dade County as a boy and as an adult. We became good friends and hunted every weekend in the 'Glades with several of the other commercial artists and cartoonists living in Miami.

Remembering Pat's and my experience on Key Biscayne during our honeymoon, I was certain Russ would be familiar with the island, and with the lone Spanish style house in the coconut grove. The house most certainly was there when he was growing up and exploring the area.

I told him of Pat's and my adventure. He seemed surprised when I referred to the lady who had befriended us when we so desperately needed help. Russ asked if I was sure this occurred on Key Biscayne across from Miami. He thought for a moment and said, "J.T., there couldn't have been anybody living there. That old house has been abandoned as far back as I can remember. It had all but fallen down, and was mostly covered over with wild vines and brush, years before the bridge was built."

Lucille, what do you know about this?

Chapter 9

MEXICO, BLOOD, AND SHARKS

Reflecting back on the major adventures of my life, I am amazed at the insignificant facts and trivial circumstances which triggered them. Certainly the great shark fishing expedition to Salina Cruz is a perfect example.

My old military buddy, Bob Hager, returned from Korea in '59 and requested an assignment at Pinecastle Air Force Base near Orlando. Pinecastle was located in the central part of the state, and that made it easy for him to visit Pat and me on weekends and holidays. We lived in Ocala, and I was the art director for a newspaper chain's Sunday-supplement magazine.

Bob and I fished, raced boats, and scouted the backcountry of the state with the same enthusiasm we had while rambling around Hokkaido back in '45 and '46. At every opportunity, we were off exploring the lakes, rivers, and swamps from the Okefenokee Swamp located on the Florida-Georgia border, to the Florida Keys. That utopian existence lasted until Pat introduced Bob to her other sister, Kay, who had recently graduated as a nurse. She was exceptionally pretty so ol' Bob's interest suddenly shifted to dating, fishing, boat racing, and exploring, and in that order, until he became my brother-in-law.

After Bob and Kay married, he left the Air Force and returned to the family farm in Illinois, and then they moved back to Sarasota where he went into construction. Within a short time, he developed a successful business. I returned to Sarasota with Pat where I published trade publications, as well as a social magazine for the area. Bob became my partner in the magazine. We never made any money, but we fished and practiced our new domestic roles as husbands and fathers.

Lucille was happy, particularly with the domestic part. She complained occasionally about the speed at which I drove, and the risk of fishing in thunderstorms, but she was generally content. She thought I should be more domestic. I suppose if I had been anyone else, I would have been content to motor along with the status quo, but there is something primitive in my genes, which calls for periodic adventure.

The great shark expedition was born while Bob and I were fishing for tarpon at 3:00 a.m. on the Myakka River, in a drizzling rain that had every indication of lasting two or three days. We weren't catching anything, which was normal tarpon fishing for me. Although I have fished thousands of hours and distinguished myself on committees for tarpon tournaments, I have never put one in the boat. I speculated on the merit of fishing for shark, but rejected the idea because the only sharks in the river were small nurse sharks, and they were about as exciting to catch as a sack of mud.

Bob said, "You talking about sharks reminds me of something I read in a magazine when I was in Korea. I think it was in a *Field and Stream* or *Sports Afield,* or something like that. The article was about a small fishing village on the southwest coast of Mexico, down near the Guatemalan border. The writer said they had the biggest sharks in the western hemisphere. The article said those monsters come right into shore to feed on the fish scraps discarded from a commercial fish processing plant."

Bob's commentary was the most exciting thing that had happened that night. I asked, "What was the name of the village?"

He didn't remember. I asked how big the sharks were and how they caught them. He wasn't sure, and said he was called on a mission and hadn't finished the article. I told him I hated unfinished stories.

He adjusted the drag on his line and mumbled, "Me too."

The drizzling rain continued. Daybreak slowly changed the sky from black to a dreary gray. I fantasized one of those giant Mexican sharks taking the bait and running. A fisherman would need three hundred yards of stainless steel line, as well as a big tarpon rig, to hold a seven-or-eight-hundred-pound fish.

I told Bob, "I bet I could land one of those rascals if I had the chance."

He asked, "What?"

I said, "One of those big Mexican sharks."

Bob turned around, facing me. "Glisson, gees, you're at it again. You're thinking about going down there?" I hadn't been, but the question was the birth of the idea.

The visitor's magazine we published regularly received letters from agencies representing airlines, offering to swap air travel for advertising space. They were called exchange vouchers. We sat another hour in the slow drizzling rain, nothing stirring, including our baited fishing lines. I asked, "Bob, if I can put it together, you want to go?"

He shrugged his shoulders and opened the palms of his hands in a melodramatic gesture. "I guess I might as well."

Lucille began grumbling somewhere in the recesses of my mind, but I didn't bother to listen.

The rest was easy; at least the ticketing was. Two weeks later, I received two round-trip air tickets, first class, Tampa to Mexico City. I also received two Mexican International rail tickets to a town called Tehuantepec, the closest rail stop to Salina Cruz, which was where the big sharks were.

We convinced our wives that we needed the experience, and they helped us each to pack an extra shirt, two pairs of socks, and our one fishing rod, which had been bought at a garage sale. It was big enough to land a Mack truck. In addition, we carried survival rations, which consisted of two jars of peanut butter, in the event we were stranded in some remote place.

The flight across the gulf in an old gas-engine Constellation was uneventful until we started to climb up and over the rim of the crater that surrounds Mexico City. A ring of thunderheads, some extending up forty thousand feet, surrounded the city. The pilot, with typical Latin bravado, augured straight into the lower third of the storm. I suspected he didn't have enough fuel to divert to another field, and the old bird's ceiling did not allow climbing over the weather. The Connie snapped up and then fell like a rock, recovered, only to repeat the maneuver again and again. Lucille was strangely absent. I assumed she had chosen to fly solo. The smell of sick passengers in second class drifted through the cabin, mixed with what I hoped was not high-octane fuel.

We finally touched down with a sickening thud, bounced off twice, and skidded to a stop. The pilot opened the compartment door to the cabin and turned, facing us. He grinned and held up two fingers, duplicating Churchill's victory salute, then shook hands with the copilot who appeared surprised to be on the ground and alive.

The steward, with composed presence, announced in Spanish and broken English, "Ladies and gentlemen, welcome to Mexico City. There will now be a small delay. The pilot informs me that we must wait here on the taxiway until the rain subsides enough to make it possible to locate the terminal."

Bob nudged me with his elbow and asked, "Glisson, tell me. Is this just the beginning or the end of the good part of this trip?"

Lucille suddenly appeared and offered to help me get reservations back to Tampa on the evening flight.

Two hours after landing, we boarded the Mexican National Railway. We then began our overnight passage, which was a ten-thousand-foot descent to Vera Cruz, which is on the Gulf of Mexico. The old steam locomotive struggled to restrain the eleven passenger cars. We twisted and turned through jagged volcanic rock, often slowing the train to three or four miles an hour. Steam mixed with the moonlit clouds, while the brakes and whistles echoed through the mountains. I have always loved trains; I stayed up all night enjoying the ride.

Bob and I arrived in Vera Cruz shortly after noon. The city was old by American standards, laid-back, and beautiful. A pervasive feeling of warmth and hospitality created a festive atmosphere, which had been conspicuously absent back in Mexico City. It was obvious American tourists were an uncommon occurrence. Twenty children surrounded us and escorted us to the stationmaster.

The stationmaster shuffled all the paper on his desk, stacked it into neat piles, and then informed us we would have a twenty-eight-hour layover. We would then board our special coach on a narrow-gauge track, and the coach would take us across the isthmus to the town of Tehuantepec. He reaffirmed there was no train to Salina Cruz, but he was confident the stationmaster in Tehuantepec would arrange transportation to our final destination.

The stationmaster seemed quite concerned about our first-class tickets. His English was terrible, and of course our Spanish was confined to sixteen words collectively. There was something about the preparation of our car, but we were not to worry. He could be relied on to solve the dilemma. He told us because of the delay in connections, the railway had arranged hotel accommodations as their guests in a local hotel. I asked Bob if he understood what the man had said.

Bob drawled, "Glisson, they have always got us to where we were going, and we have always managed to get back. Besides, if they screw up, we can't get our money back since we didn't pay anything in the first place."

We spent the night in a local hotel and slept until mid- morning. Breakfast was served on a balcony surrounded with red bougainvillea and cascades of flame vines. In addition to dining on various tropical fruits, we added the seventeenth word—chicken—to our Spanish vocabulary, "pollo," a word that came in handy before the expedition ended.

Twenty-eight hours and thirty minutes after we arrived, the train to Tehuantepec pulled out of Vera Cruz with Bob and me residing alone in the most luxurious car either of us could possibly imagine. It had deep oriental carpets, velvet drapes with gold tassels, marble tabletops, and a marble-and-mahogany bar. I tried to go forward and ask where the car came from, and why we were in it alone. The door was locked.

I told Bob, "We are locked in here. Why do you suppose they did that?"

He said, "Glisson, it's probably to protect big shots like us from banditos who rob folks that ride in rigs like this." We examined a velvet cord, adorned with gold bric-a-brac, hanging near his lounge chair. I suggested Bob pull it and see what would happen. He told me he calculated one of three things. "It may stop the train, it may unhitch this car from the train, or possibly fumigate this rolling palace."

He pulled the cord. Chimes dinged and donged throughout the coach and a porter promptly appeared from a compartment behind the bar.

"Do you speak English?" we asked simultaneously.

He said, "Yes, Señor. Can I be of service?"

Before Bob could get his first question out, I asked, "Why are we in this private car? Do all visitors to Mexico get such grand treatment?"

His answer was more like the tone of the concierge at New York Plaza than a railroad conductor. "You are modest, sir. You and your friend are special guests of the country. I believe you use the term V.I.P."

After a dozen questions, the situation became clearer. The airline that arranged the trip in exchange for our tickets had exaggerated our status. We were publishers from the States who had come to Mexico to possibly do a series of travel articles on the wonders of the country. They had our tickets marked as special dignitaries. In addition, the Mexican Tourist Bureau had been a model of efficiency, notifying everyone along our route to provide its most deluxe accommodations.

Apparently, no one could guess why we had chosen Salina Cruz as our destination, and the word had gone out for everyone to provide the best accommodations. We had drinks and settled in to enjoy the accommodations and status, even if it was more than questionable.

Our dignitary status appeared to expire simultaneously with our arrival in Tehuantepec at 3:33 a.m. A solitary bulb mounted on a wooden pole cast a red glow over and around what appeared to be the station, which was the only structure in a landscape of red sand and dust. Six or seven passengers got off the train and immediately disappeared into the darkness. The train moved out without bells or whistle, leaving nothing but silence.

A dilapidated prewar Chevrolet with a luggage rack on top sat at the outer perimeter of the light. I wondered if it had been abandoned there several months ago, or if it was a historic symbol of transportation in the province.

We both stood in the same spot where we had stepped down from the train. The bats swishing in and out around the lighted pole, the abandoned station, the old Chevrolet, and Bob standing there holding our eight-foot fishing rod and reel in the middle of a desert, provided credibility for the nonexistent reality of the moment. I said, "What do you think, Bob?" and immediately felt stupid for asking.

He said, "Looks like the cactus have all starved to death " He turned his head in every direction without moving his shoulders. "Glisson, it don't look like much for fishing here." He touched his forehead with his index finger, feigning deep concentration. "I believe our best first move is to find an ocean, and if we expect to accomplish that, we are going to need some qualified help."

We picked up our bags and started walking in the direction where the passengers had disappeared when we were suddenly immersed in the headlights of the old car. They dimmed as the starter on the old Chevrolet brought the engine coughing and spitting into life. We both let out a whoop and ran to the vehicle.

Bob shouted, "Can we hire you to take us to Salina Cruz?"

I suggested, "Maybe you could take us to a place where there is a taxi."

The driver pried the door open and squeezed out. "You are Señor Hager and Señor Glisson, the Americanos?"

Shaking our heads like two puppets on the same string, we shouted, "Yes!"

The man, who was no more than five feet in height, buttoned his faded blue coat and extended his hand. "I am Juan Carlos Aguilar. I wait for you since we get the message from Vera Cruz yesterday. I am sorry, but I am asleep when the train comes." He made a sweeping gesture with his right hand. "Welcome to Salina Cruz. I take you there now." He caressed our fishing rod as if it was a work of fine art, then tied it to the rack on top of the car.

We crowded into the front seat and were off in a cloud of smoke and dust. The dash had more religious ornamentation than the Catholic Basilica back in St Augustine. In addition to a saint in a seashell, there were two Saint Christopher statues, a plastic Virgin Mary, and several commemorative metals glued to the windshield. These were all under a string of pink tassels suspended across the top of the windshield.

I told Lucille, "This is your kind of car."

She was insulted and replied, "Mr. Aguilar will need a lot of divine help to drive and see through all that collective security."

"How far is it to Salina Cruz?" I asked.

Juan Carlos answered, "Maybe twenty kilometers. Don't you worry Señor, Juan Carlos Aguilar takes care of everything for you, except catching the giant shark." He laughed until his laughter was consumed by a cough, aggravated by the mixture of oil, smoke and dust boiling up through the floorboard, not to mention the cigarette clinging to his lower lip. He took both hands off the steering wheel and waved his arms in a magnanimous gesture. "I have notified everyone of your arrival and they are happy to meet you."

Bob asked, effecting confused sincerity, "Glisson, where did we go wrong? He, and probably the whole town, maybe the whole country, thinks we are somebody important."

I shouted back, "It has to be the airline that arranged the trip. Everything is first class."

Bob said, "Including this Salina Cruz limousine?"

Juan Carlos answered for me, "Si, Señor. It is first class."

The great shark fishing expedition of 1959 rolled into Salina Cruz at ten after four in the morning. Bob and I, and, of course, Juan Carlos Aguilar, were the only life forms awake. There were two dim streetlights, and an intense white light coming from a one-story building, which had double doors open to the dirt street.

Juan Carlos brought his vehicle to a stop directly in front of the door. He had pulled two wheels up onto the sidewalk.

"This, Señors, is the Hotel Salina Cruz. It is the finest hotel in the city." He grinned. "It is also the only hotel in the city." He stepped out and spoke in a tone half way between a request and an order, "You wait here." And then he ran into the hotel. A flood of electrifying Spanish conversation followed, includ-

GIBSON

ing words like "Americanos," "Glisson," "Hager," and "importante." After an extended discussion that surely woke half the residents of the town, Juan Carlos came running out, followed by a man brushing his hair in place with his hands, and a lady in a black uniform attempting to tie on a little white apron. A confusing rattle of introductions followed, while our driver and self-appointed escort took our overnight bags and gave one to the man and the other to the lady who was still having trouble tying her apron. Juan Carlos led the way into the hotel.

The lobby was about twelve feet by twelve, painted light green, with a light green tile floor. There was a small desk and a potted palm that needed water, and most conspicuous, a five-hundred-fifty-watt bulb glaring from the ceiling.

Our room, directly off the lobby, had snow-white plaster walls, a spring green tile floor, and two single beds made of ponderosa pine finished with clear varnish. The beds were made with immaculate white sheets tucked in, hospital-style. There was a small table, a straight chair, and another single glaring light bulb suspended from the ceiling.

The floors and bare walls reverberated the smallest sound. Juan Carlos appeared to be making a speech in Mexican-English, extolling the hospitality of Salina Cruz, while the manager and maid were both speaking Spanish at the speed of sound. Suddenly, the three of them fell quiet. As they backed out of the room, they said, "Buenos noches!"

The silence was short-lived. Within seconds, every rooster south of Brownsville started crowing at once.

Bob said, "Glisson, you stay up and keep the chickens happy. I'm going to sleep."

I ignored Lucille's negative comments and drifted off to sleep, savoring the moment. We were at the right place and hopefully at the right time. Very possibly we were on the threshold of catching the biggest shark south of the North Pole.

The international sound of children playing and dogs barking provided the conversion from deep sleep to consciousness before I opened my eyes. I was temporarily blinded by the glare of sunlight coming through the room's only window. Bob sat up and looked at his watch. He spoke like a military commander.

"Glisson, let's move it. It is nearly noon and we haven't caught a shark yet."

We showered and shaved in cold water, dressed, and rushed out to survey Salina Cruz, and to catch the biggest shark in southern Mexico.

Juan Carlos was sleeping in his car in the exact place he parked the night before. The hotel manager rushed past the two of us and banged on the hood of the old Chevrolet. Juan Carlos sprang from the car, tucking in his shirt with one hand and brushing his hair with the other. "Good morning, Señor Hager. Good morning, Señor Glisson. Juan Carlos is at your service. I have arranged for you to meet the champion shark fisherman of Salina Cruz. You will learn all there is to know about such sport, but first you must have the breakfast I prepare for you."

I said, "Are you buying us breakfast?"

He laughed until it turned into the rasping cough. "No, Señor, but I get the best price for you."

Bob said, "Come on, Glisson. Let's eat breakfast. He is probably the only person in five hundred miles that can understand your southern drawl."

We dined in a walled-in patio, on papayas, melon, and hard- boiled eggs. I skipped the coffee that could have melted a nail. When we finished, Juan Carlos announced that it was siesta time and we should rest until three o'clock. We both protested, pointing out we had been up less than a hour. "But Señor, it is twelve o'clock. Everyone takes the siesta now. I pick you up here at the hotel at exactly three o'clock, and we go visit the fishing expert." He tipped the air where his hat would have been if he had one, and left the patio.

We decided to check out the town on our own. Salina Cruz was no more than a village by the ocean. There were two general stores, a pharmacy, ice cream and tobacco shop, and a cantina, which served only beer and soft drinks. These were all built around a park with no grass, but with an imposing granite pedestal whose statue politics or scoundrels had caused to be removed. The houses were mostly made of terra-cotta blocks, plastered over with stucco. Only two houses on a hillside had typical Spanish terra-cotta roofs; the rest were small and flat.

We walked to the shoreline. West of the village, a massive jetty extended half a mile, directly out into the Pacific Ocean. To the north, there was a harbor protected from the ocean by a peninsula on the west side, leaving a narrow channel between it and the jetty. We later learned the jetty was built by the Americans to create an alternative port at the Mexican isthmus, should the Panama Canal be closed for any reason. Commercial fishing boats were anchored at the upper end of the harbor near what we assumed was a seafood-processing house. A single dirt road connected the village to the docks and processing facility. As we looked toward the docks, no boat or man was moving.

Back toward the village, there was no one in sight. I told Bob, "These people sure take their siesta seriously." He suggested all the people had evacuated the area until the two gringo shark fisherman left town.

Only small children and dogs began to move shortly after three o'clock. At four o'clock, the women came out of their houses, shopping at vegetable stands which had miraculously appeared in the town center, along with vendors selling pots and pans and hand-made furniture.

At four-thirty even, Juan Carlos emerged from his taxi, reflecting near panic. He said we must go quickly for our appointment with his fishing expert. Twenty kids appeared out of nowhere, staring at us as if we were the strangest sight they had ever seen. I asked Juan, "What do they want?"

He answered, spreading his arms as if he were addressing a stadium crowd, "They come to see you, señor. You are the Americanos who will catch the great shark tomorrow morning." He spoke to them in Spanish, saying something that caused them to make expressions of amazement at the end of each sentence. When he finished, they jumped up and down and gave us, or someone, a rousing cheer. Juan insisted we sit in the back seat, mumbling something about dignity or dignitary.

The children ran alongside the old Chevrolet, cheering in the dust and smoke, until we turned onto a road that meandered up through a narrow gully. This led to a modest little cottage surrounded by stacks of what appeared to be crab traps.

An old man who reflected the weathering of many years at sea sat on the porch mending a fish net with a net needle. He waved and motioned us to come in before Juan Carlos stopped the car. With sincerity he said, "Buenos dias. Welcome."

We introduced ourselves before Juan Carlos could take over as master of ceremonies. "I am Jose Diaz, 'Joe,' to my American friends. And I say again, you are most welcome." He motioned in the direction of two boxes. "Come sit in the shade, and we will talk of Florida and how you knew of a place so insignificant as Salina Cruz."

The visit with Joe Diaz was the first sane thing that had happened since we left Tampa. He told us of working on freighters that took him to four continents, and of fishing vessels large and small. He asked about our families and homes, and told us of growing up on the Pacific coast of Mexico.

He saw us sneaking glimpses at the sun and said, "There is no hurry my friends. Juan Carlos tells me you would like to catch one of the big sharks that comes into the pass at the end of the jetty."

I asked if he could help us.

He answered, "I can tell you how to hook one if you have luck, but I cannot tell you how to land one." He paused for a few seconds. "I am too old and crippled to help you, and to be honest, I think it may be impossible to land one with hand-held gear." Our disappointment was obvious. He laughed, "But it could be damn good sport to try!"

Joe Diaz laid out the plan: first, we needed to attract the shark to come in close to the jetty. To do that, we should go to the slaughterhouse at the edge of town and get five gallons of blood to put into the water on the outgoing tide. Because there was no refrigeration, cows and goats were killed after midnight for consumption the following day.

Juan Carlos said, "I have taken the liberty to make the arrangement with the butcher to have the blood ready for you to pick up at four o'clock in the morning."

Joe Diaz decided, after studying a tide chart, six thirty was the perfect time to attract the fish. He suggested Juan Carlos help us purchase two live chickens from a local housewife for bait.

Bob said, "Now, at six-thirty in the morning we are at the end of the jetty, we have five gallons of blood and two chickens, then what do we do?"

Señor Diaz answered, "Put the blood into the water a little at a time in a spot where the tide is running out. I believe it will be best if you tie the hook and line to the chicken's legs, leaving the wings free to flap. If you imbed the hook, the chicken will be injured and not be very active."

He paused, giving us an opportunity to clear up anything we didn't understand. He continued, "Then you wait for the shark. If you are lucky, several will come. I suggest you continue to put the blood in the water until they have developed a great appetite, then throw the chicken into the water. You will need to have the drag set down as tight as the reel will take it without burning it up."

"And be sure you position yourself behind one of the big rocks where you can brace your feet before you set the hook." He thought for a minute. "I regret I can not come with you. It will be a moment you will not soon forget."

Lucille grabbed onto the part about having my feet behind a rock. She reminded me that I could get another opportunity to water ski barefoot with the added thrill of being pulled by a man-eating shark.

The rest of the day was like something from an Italian opera. A large crowd gathered in the town square, and especially in and around the ice cream shop. When we asked Juan why, he answered with his usual theatrical gestures,

"Señor, because it is a celebration. A celebration for the men who will catch the big shark tomorrow."

Bob said, "Glisson, do you suppose there is any way we could leave for the States right now?" Before I could answer he continued, "This is going to be like the water ski show at Cypress Gardens." Then he added, "Probably worse."

Lucille asked if I knew the shortest route to a hospital that treated shark bites. I ignored her and reminded Bob it was he who brought up the idea of shark fishing in Mexico. He said he was glad he didn't tell me about the article he read on walruses at the South Pole.

When we stepped out of Juan's taxi, the people applauded, and with Juan's help, we were literally pushed into the ice cream shop. Customers got up and offered us a seat along the wall. When we sat down, two large ladies old enough to be our mothers took seats next to us. There were a dozen or more pretty girls in the shop, and no men except Juan.

The proprietor came over and gave each of us a large paper cone with two scoops of lime-flavored ice cream. The girls all licked their ice cream, staring at us and smiling occasionally, doing both with an air of practiced sophistication. Juan broke into one of his discourses which we couldn't understand and which the ladies seemed to ignore.

Some of the girls were quite beautiful. When one looked directly at Bob and smiled, it prompted another large lady to squeeze in between us. Juan Carlos explained, "The señoras are the mothers and chaperones." It was the first time I had ever seen ol' Bob blush. We sat for ten awkward minutes trying to eat the ice cream as fast as possible without our heads splitting. Finally, we thanked the proprietor and said good night. Juan announced, "We must go now."

Night came while we were inside, and when we stepped out of the doorway, we were blinded by the darkness. Juan Carlos said the reason you come to this shop is because here in this town, it is necessary to pay respect to the ladies. Now that is finished and we go and have a good time." He led us in the opposite direction from the hotel, along with all the men that had been gathered outside the ice cream shop. We followed a path up over a hill, away from any of the lights of Salina Cruz. I told Bob I wished I knew where we were going.

He said, "Don't worry. Ol' Juan is in charge. He's a one-man, self-appointed guide, transportation director, mayor, and God-only-knows-what-else."

A quarter-mile through the darkness, we came to a building with no outside lights. Someone opened a door and we all poured in. The place was illuminated with neon beer signs and a lantern. It was smoky, crowded, and loud. I didn't know what they called a place like it in Mexico, but if it were in Florida, it would be called a juke joint. A man with a large hat played an ancient handmade wooden xylophone. I would like to have heard it if there had not been so much noise.

We drank tequila, beer, and something Juan said was special from the area. It was a clear liquid, thick as cane syrup. He said if we had more than two drinks of the special brew, we could catch sharks with our bare hands. There were only two women in the place. They occasionally tried to dance, but gave up because of the lack of space. Drinking seemed to be the object of all the patrons. Bob asked Juan if it was like this every night. He said no. This was a special celebration for the shark fishermen.

The high point of the evening came when a man burst in the door, shouting and waving a live chicken and a duck over his head. Every one shouted, "Tiburo'n tarnada!"

Juan translated: "Shark bait!"

The duck and hen were passed from one person to another, and finally presented to us, flapping and fluttering. Even though their feet were bound, they were free to squawk and quack and flap their wings. Bob asked why he had brought a duck instead of two chickens. Juan gestured and said something like, "No important."

Feathers floated in the murky light. We drank with one hand and restrained the bait with the other. Juan Carlos yelled above the noise, "It is a good party, yes?" I asked him whom we should pay for the birds. He said they were a gift from the men of Salina Cruz. I suspected the birds' real owners did not know they had donated the chicken or the duck.

Bob leaned over so he could shout in my ear, "Glisson, the odds are two to one if we don't make Juan Carlos take the bait back to the hotel now, one of two things will happen. We will be cleaning up chicken or duck do, or worse, we could be the first Americans arrested in southern Mexico as chicken thieves." We convinced our faithful guide and newfound friend to bid all our guests good night, and carried the chicken and the duck back to the hotel.

At one o'clock, we made it back to our room. We put the chicken and the duck in the shower, and fell into bed. We had a three a.m. wake-up call, a promise made by both the manager and Juan Carlos.

The manager woke us promptly at three.

Bob rolled out of bed and pointed to the ceiling. "Get up, Glisson! For this is it, the time to go forth and collect the blood to slay the mighty sharks that strike fear in the hearts of the good people of Salina Cruz."

We discovered a duck or chicken egg in the shower, then went out front and woke Juan Carlos from a sound sleep in the taxi.

I have been in unpleasant places, but none so unpleasant as a Mexican small town slaughterhouse at four in the morning. Juan insisted upon introducing Bob and me to everyone there. They in turn all insisted on shaking our hands and, because of their friendship with our guide, they gave us double the amount of blood we asked for: two, five-gallon tin containers with no handles.

Bob and I did a balancing act on the back seat of the taxi, holding the blood buckets on our laps while Juan drove back to the hotel. The lady who couldn't tie her apron had prepared a breakfast including our bonus egg from the shower. Unfortunately, after our visit to the slaughterhouse, neither of us had an appetite. We chose to sit on the curb and wait for daylight and destiny. Bob said he sure hoped no one was up so we could try our luck without an audience. I agreed.

Dawn broke somewhere back in the direction of Tehuantepec and Tampa. Bob and I gathered our fishing rig, the chicken and the duck, climbed in the taxi for the two-block trip across town to the end of the jetty. The entire town was already out there or on the way. We squeezed past individuals and families carrying little babies. They all nodded and waved as if we were old friends. Juan eased the old Chevrolet down the narrow pass way built along the top of the giant gray rocks. When we reached the end, we got out and surveyed the situation.

The jetty was made of rocks, four to eight feet in diameter, piled six feet above the normal high tide line. A one-or-two-mile wind created a light ripple on the murky blue water. Juan guessed the water was about twelve feet deep. There was a slight current flowing out toward the open ocean along the harbor side of the jetty.

Bob said, "Ol' buddy, like they say back home, it's time to fish or cut bait. Let's get at it."

I started pouring the blood into the water. Ten minutes later, there had been no sign of big fish. I poured the second bucket in, more slowly. We waited and nothing happened.

Several teenage boys dove into the water and pried oysters loose from the rocks, and then passed them up to the people on the jetty. I was alarmed. I told Juan to tell them to get out of the water, that the sharks would be coming.

He said, "It is O.K., Señor. They know the ocean and when to get out."

Suddenly, a hundred feet from the end of the jetty, the water broke and a huge blue-gray shape rose to the surface. I thought it was the biggest critter since Jonah's whale. Bob was staring with his mouth open. I do not know why I grabbed the fishing rod, certainly not to fish with, more likely as something with which to defend myself. I looked around and saw everyone was laughing. It was a manta ray more than twelve feet across. It rolled past the end of the jetty, followed by another about the same size.

Bob laughed, "Glisson, I thought the same thing you did when it first broke the surface. I thought it was a shark, and believe me if one comes by here with a head as wide as that thing, I'll be back in Sarasota before I stop."

We sat for a few minutes relaxing. I don't know if I really expected a big shark to show up or not. Someone yelled, "There!" Then everyone was yelling and pointing. Three fins cut the surface two hundred feet out from the jetty. I grabbed the chicken from the trunk of the taxi and looped the line around its legs, with the hook dangling just below the feet. I soused the chicken in the blood and drew back to throw it into the water, in the direction of the shark. Bob had the rod. He yelled, "Wait! Don't throw it until they come close."

They made a pass about fifty feet out and disappeared. A few seconds passed when one rolled no more than ten feet from the rocks. I heaved the chicken; it fell eight feet from the rocks. A second shark ran at the flopping bait from maybe fifteen feet out. The monstrous jaws came open and the chicken disappeared. Bob made a mighty heave to set the hook while the line was running out. He reeled it in with only the chicken's legs and a naked hook. He threw down the rod, stomped the rocks and let loose the ultimate of his profane vocabulary, "Confound it! Dang it! Dang!"

Juan came charging across the rocks and thrust the old duck into my hands. "Here, Señor, put it on the line. Be quick! They are there, yes? Down there, si."

I dunked the old bird into the last of the blood in the bucket and handed the duck to Bob. He said, "Thanks for putting the blood on before we tie the hooks on her." He raised the wings and wrapped the line just behind the duck's breast, securing the hook on the underside of the duck's belly while she flopped, sprinkling the two of us from head to foot with red spatters of blood. The only movement in the water was the lazy swirl of several white chicken feathers in the outgoing tide. Bob heaved the duck in their general direction.

When it hit the water, both sharks ran for it. Their mouths came open and they rolled belly up, prepared to devour the duck, but this time it was not so easy. The old bird flapped its wings and rose off the water just enough. Both of the sharks missed, then circled short and made another try. One lunged with half his body coming out of the water, sending an avalanche of spray into the air, obscuring the duck for a moment. I waited for the line to tighten, but when the spray cleared, the duck was flapping toward the jetty. The townspeople cheered. The biggest shark made another try and the old bird evaded him again. Now the people were shouting "Ole!" They were clearly shouting for the duck. If I tightened the line I could force the duck onto the water pulling it backward. I didn't have the heart. It was a fair contest.

The sharks made two more passes while the whole town shouted "Ole!" and other encouragement. The duck made a final lunge and waddled up onto the rocks. A mighty cheer went up for Salina Cruz' valiant duck. Everyone ran to the victor. They held her up like a trophy for every one to see. The last Bob and I saw of our bait, it was cradled in the arm of one of the matronly chaperones who had protected the virtue of the girls the night before. She was striding down the jetty toward the town.

Juan Carlos was ecstatic. "Señors, it was a good show, yes? Maybe the best I have seen."

In a soft deliberate tone, Bob asked, "When is the next train back to Mexico City?"

Juan answered, "It leaves Tehuantepec at three thirty, Señor. That gives us time to go to the cantina and celebrate, yes?"

We reluctantly agreed. Neither of us were real drinkers, but considering that Hemingway did that sort of thing after a battle with a giant denizen of the deep, it seemed the proper thing to do. We, and the regulars of the cantina, drank a toast to the sharks, then one to the chicken and the duck, and our host proposed a toast to the great sports fishermen of America.

Lucille asked if I had enough of shark fishing.

I said, "Why should you care?" And I added, "There was no way I could have been in danger on this trip."

Her answer was smug. "You were in danger many times, including your stance on the bloody rocks with the sharks a few inches below you."

We departed Salina Cruz shortly before three p.m., and were amazed that most of citizens, including the pretty girls and their chaperones, cut their siesta short to see us off.

I often wonder if our big-game fishing rod and reel is still hanging over the bar in the cantina that lies hidden behind the hill from Salina Cruz.

 Chapter 10

AIR MARJORIE

Motivation is an elusive urge. Hunger, sex, and fear of falling all come naturally, but motivation sneaks out when you least expect it. Motivation is not necessarily good. It frequently leads to disaster.

There were many sound reasons why I might have lived out my life without owning an airplane: the Depression, money, availability, and opportunity. However, the old Proverb, "Be careful what you pray for; you will probably get it," has consistently prevailed in my life, possibly from Lucille's influence.

For more years than I like to admit, I have flown just about every type of plane that had wings and a propeller. Most of the rigs were derelicts. In retrospect, I have never owned a respectable airplane. The cheapest rentals at the airport were reserved for me. When I finally bought my first plane, it was an Air Coupe that was on the verge of being junked. It was a far cry from the sleek craft I had vowed to own. Pat named it Eddy Rickety Back. It looked so bad that the airport manager made me tie it down behind the hangar. When I had it only three months, a twister destroyed it on the ground. I suspect Lucille had something to do with its demise.

Shortly after the dissolution of Eddy Rickety Back, one of my friends formed a consortium and bought an old surplus AT-6. Everyone took turns. We flew it four weeks, and then the consortium sold it for a slight loss. It was a cheap plane, except it burned twenty gallons of gas an hour, and none of us could afford much of that. In addition, only the front seat came with it, so it was difficult to get a passenger to share the cost of flying when they found they had to sit on an orange crate belted to the floor in the rear cockpit.

In the late '50s, Pat and I visited her parents in Sarasota. I, of course, used the opportunity to visit the local airport and inspect the planes that were for sale. When I drove onto the field, a man was rolling out an all-metal Luscombe AE. He had just finished major and general restorations of the fully aerobatic little sports plane. The Luscombe boasted a new white paint job and was trimmed in fire engine red. The interior was done with light tan Mercedes leather and fabrics. Although it was built before I was born, and had more previous owners than I had cousins, it represented the fulfillment of a dream. It was the second time I fell in love in Sarasota.

I was publishing trade magazines and working on a concept for one for the doublewides (mobile homes that would be manufactured in two halves). I bought the Luscombe and named it "Luci-lu," but the name didn't stick. (Lucille didn't like the name.) My wife named it *The Gnat* because it was small, and Lucille approved. *The Gnat*'s radio call letters were, 1-8-Kilo.

Although I couldn't afford it, I justified the purchase of *The Gnat* as a vehicle that would enhance the efficiency of the trade magazines I was publishing at that time. The little jewel was small, slow, tough, and stressed for seven G's positive and four G's negative. It could be depended on to stay in one piece while skirting the thunderstorms that lay over Florida nine months of the year. It could land and take off in the high grass and water that were an accepted component of the small air strips in south and central Florida. I flew the little devil back to Leesburg.

Lucille was not pleased. She did not approve of my purchase. In fact, one of her favorite expressions was, "If man was supposed to fly, he would have been born with wings, like me."

My children tell anyone who will listen, "When we were growing up, our dad's family outings were so reckless we would run and hide when he offered to take us on one." They elaborate on long-forgotten minor storms, landslides, and near natural disasters that were frivolous when looked at in retrospect. I was doing what all good fathers should do, providing them with adventure and good experiences.

My wife said, speaking for herself and the children, "We have had more experience than we will ever use." Quite naturally, the kids' exaggerated recollections served only to heighten their mother's fear of heights, speed, darkness, reptiles, and any machine that makes more noise than a refrigerator.

In an effort to be fair, I confess that Lucille, overworked as she claims to be, has played a significant role in deflecting some incidents that threatened to get out of hand, and in some cases, threatened my survival.

I tell you this to preface an incident that occurred several years ago when my young'uns were growing up. There are those who say that my use of the word, "incident," is a gross understatement, and that I would not be telling it now if my flying license and the statute of limitations had not expired. My sister, Marjorie, tends to be more dramatic. She refers to it as that terrifying catastrophe into which I got her.

My dad told me, "Son, look out for little mistakes. They can get you the same as the big ones." The little incident with my sister and the sports plane almost did.

In the late 1950s, Marjorie and her husband lived on a farm in north central Florida, bordering the Ocala National Forest. Pat and I lived in Leesburg, a small town thirty-five miles to the south. On any occasion that I was flying in the vicinity of my sister's farm, I would descend and buzz the house, low enough to sweep the leaves and chickens from the yard. This was my way of notifying her that I intended to land on a nearby Forestry Service landing strip, and would be her guest for lunch or dinner. She would, in turn, drive to the strip and transport me to her home and table.

Marjorie was and still is the best cook I know. In addition, she is complimentary and always had nice things to say about my airplanes. That was an opinion not bestowed by pilots, aircraft mechanics, or air controllers. In return, I offered to fly my sister over the farm or make a quick circle around the field. Marjorie invariably declined, saying she was afraid of planes, and mumbling something about remembering bad experiences with me when we were kids. I always gave the invitation and she consistently refused. If I insisted she said her husband might object.

My invitations to fly (and Marjorie's rejections) might have continued interminably except for one occasion that I am reluctant to speak of until this very day.

In the sixties shortly after I purchased the Luscombe I had an early morning appointment in Gainesville that ended before ten a.m. My friend drove me back to the airport, and I took off into blue skies and puffy clouds, passing over Newnans and Lochloosa Lakes.

It was one of those beautiful days in March when spring comes early to North Florida. I did lazy S's, practiced stalls, followed a train across a trestle, flew through orange groves, and admired my reflection in a lake near Citra. Even Lucille was in a good mood. I told her, "This is what living is all about." Drifting around like a well-fed eagle, we found ourselves over my sister's farm. I remembered Pat and the boys had driven up to Marjorie's from Leesburg to spend the day. I was envious of the hospitality and incredible food they were enjoying a thousand feet below me. I pondered the situation visualizing fresh hot yeast rolls, butter beans, and candied yams. *Gnat* involuntarily banked in the direction of the farm. Business could wait.

Once the decision was made, I delighted in my good judgment. I would share in the fun, have a great meal, and show my new airplane to my favorite sister. One hundred feet over the isolated farmhouse, I cut the throttle, banked hard left, and pointed the nose at the open space behind the house. At thirty feet, I leveled out upwind, pushed the throttle to the firewall, and zoomed across the back yard with Lucille screaming louder than the engine. In my periphery, I saw kids pouring out the back door, followed by my wife and Marjorie, all waving and shouting. As I pulled up and banked back toward the house, they were all running to the car in a race to get to the little air strip in the woods before I could land and taxi up to the fence.

We arrived simultaneously. I taxied up, allowing the end of the wing to extend over the fence, shading my family. They were all talking at once and waving, while the engine idled and then fell silent.

While I pulled the chocks from the rear compartment and secured the tiny two-seater, our kids were all talking at once—"Daddy's got a new toy, but it's so small."

Marjorie's daughter, Coni, exclaimed, "Red and white is what makes it sporty." I gave it a pat on the engine cowling before joining my family over the fence.

"What do you think" I asked my sister.

She was exuberant. "It is a cute little thing. Sometime, I would even like to ride in one like that." She had established the possibility.

I jumped at the opportunity. "Get over the fence and I'll take you for a ride. There is no time like the present."

The children all chanted, "Do it, Aunt Marjorie. Do it!"

She retreated to the car saying, "Maybe after lunch. We have to get back to the house before lunch gets cold." The kids let out a common groan and we all climbed into the station wagon.

Over fresh garden vegetables, roast beef, and conversation about small airplanes, I stressed the safety features of the Luscombe, in a deliberate attempt to build confidence in my passenger-to-be.

The kids continued to sing, "Aunt Marjorie is going fly with Dad-dy."

She whispered a low, "Maybe."

When lunch was finally concluded, I told Marjorie that I hated to eat and run, but I should be getting back to Leesburg before sundown.

With a look of foreboding, Marjorie said, "We will run you back to your plane."

Following their singing, "Aunt Marjorie is going to flyeee," the kids continued with their version of *The Man On The Flying Trapeze.*

When we arrived at the strip, everyone poured out of the car, yelling, "Come on Aunt Marjorie. We'll help you over the fence."

Sitting there in the forest, glittering in the afternoon sun, the little plane looked like a surrealist's impression of restrained motion. The grass strip was less than sixty feet wide, boxed in on four sides with ancient live oaks and pine trees.

Marjorie reluctantly climbed the fence, saying "I will take a look, and then we'll see." The kids and Pat all applauded and cheered. I pointed out the all-metal fuselage, the tan leather seats, and phosphorous-coated instruments which glowed in the dark.

"Get in," I urged. "Just step up on that chrome foothold and slip into the seat. Here, let me help you." She hesitated, then she stepped up and in.

I immediately locked the acrobatic restraint belt and secured the door on her side.

Marjorie said, "It is so small. I think I want to get out." I assured her everything was fine. I had the feeling Lucille had crossed over and was trying to talk her out of going.

The kids yelled, "Go, Aunt Marjorie! Go!"

I was sure she would love it once we were soaring in the wild blue yonder. I ran around to the pilot's side to prepare for takeoff, reached in, opened the throttle, and checked to see if the switch was closed.

"What are you doing?" she asked.

"Just sit still while I prop it,", I ordered.

"What do you mean, prop it?" she snapped.

"Pull the propeller to crank it," I answered.

Her voice became high pitched. "You mean you don't have a starter in this thing? I want to get out!"

I was desperate not to lose my passenger. "It'll only take a few seconds and then you will love it."

I ran to the front and pulled the prop through until I heard the carburetor sucking gas. Then I ran back to the cockpit and shut off the throttle and opened the switch. I pulled the prop. It was supposed to crank. It didn't. I came back, reached in and closed the switch and reopened the throttle. Then I raced back and pulled the propeller again to suck more gas into the engine. I knew the engines could be cantankerous when they were warm. I glanced at my sister. She was weaving back and forth, trying to unhitch the restraints.

The kids yelled, "Don't get out, Aunt Marjorie! It'll start."

She said, half pleading, "That is what I am afraid of."

I raced from the propeller to the cockpit. Lucille was shouting, "Not today." I ignored her, turned the switch off, and opened the throttle. I pulled the prop, went back, closed the throttle, and opened the switch. Then I spun the prop, closed the throttle, opened the switch, closed the switch, closed the throttle, and pulled the prop. Finally, in my desperation to make the stubborn engine start, I made a critical mistake. I flipped the switch on, and left the throttle wide open.

I barely moved the propeller. The powerful little plane exploded into life, jumping the chocks, and forcing me to fall backward to escape the whirling propeller. The throttle was wide open. The engine would pull the plane into the air in seconds. As the plane roared past, I grabbed the wing strut and tried to hold it back. A second later, I was making ten-foot steps trying to keep up. It was worse than any nightmare.

With one hand, I got the door open that had blown shut, and with my other hand, I desperately tried to get to the switch or to the throttle. They were out of reach. If I released my grip on the wing strut, the plane would soar into the air with my sister, and meet certain disaster. Marjorie was no help. She had her hands over her eyes and was screaming as loud as the engine. I felt something stinging the side of my face, but certainly had no time to investigate.

In what I believed was my last desperate attempt, I hit the plexiglass window with my fist and broke through to the throttle. The sudden silence was awesome. I tried to look around, and found myself in heavy underbrush beneath huge live oaks. It took a few seconds to gain some semblance of orientation. While I had held the strut on one side, the plane was forced to turn and head directly into the woods, at a right angle to the runway.

Total silence continued to permeate the hammock. Anything capable of making noise had been paralyzed. Marjorie sat like a white mannequin, staring blankly into space. The airstrip was not in sight. The propeller had cut a curving path through the scrub oaks into the hammock, barely missing several large trees. I climbed under the fuselage to the passenger side and pried the door open, forcing the brush back from the plane.

The first worldly sounds came from Pat and the kids, scrambling through the brush calling, "Where are you? Are you OK, Aunt Marjorie?" The voices seemed to bring her back to reality.

She turned her head slowly toward me and said, "Is it over?"

I said, "Let me help you out." She nodded in agreement. I unlatched the shoulder harness and helped her down. When her legs reached the ground they were of no use. Her knees buckled, causing her to sink to the ground. I lifted her several times before they would support her weight.

One of the boys said, "Dad, did you intend to do that with your plane?"

I gave him a dirty look and said, "No," as softly as possible.

Marjorie, acting like someone who had returned from the dead, began to hug the kids and Pat. Then she asked, "Can I go home now?"

When we arrived back at the house, Marjorie said, "Don't tell my husband. He won't understand."

The next day, I beat the propeller back into the general shape it was originally, put masking tape over the tears in the wings, and flew the plane to a friend's repair facility at the Ocala airport. I didn't feel Lucille's presence on the flight. I knew she was back up there trying to resign or get transferred again.

I think my sister would have forgiven me if I had not pushed my luck a little too far. When *The Gnat* was repaired, I flew back up to the farm. Marjorie came down and picked me up.

In retrospect, I believe Lucille caused me to say, "Marjorie, if you are good to me and fix me a good lunch, I'll take you up and fly you over the farm."

She said in a soft, calculated voice, "Don't you, ever, ever, mention the word, 'flying,' to me again."

I nearly missed a good dinner and a ride back to my plane.

Thankfully, Pat and the children were far enough from the runaway Luscombe to miss the seriousness of the moment. They thought I was doing it as a joke and could not hear Marjorie's screaming above the roar of the engine. Pat said it was like what she had come to call "another one of those Glisson things."

To her and the kids, the whole episode appeared to be more like the Keystone Cops in slow motion than a near tragedy. They continued to fly with me. My sister was not so forgiving.

There was one other episode in the Luscombe that is worth mentioning. That summer, Pat became pregnant again. It was our last chance to have a girl, and we anxiously awaited the coming event. Three of the boys had been born in Sarasota, and one in Ocala.

Like most women, Pat was fond of the obstetrician who had delivered her first-born, as well as the third and fourth sons, in Sarasota. She reluctantly went to an obstetrician in Leesburg. I thought she was happy with the local physician, and I assumed our fifth child would be born in Leesburg. However, when she knew the time had come, she told me, "Today is the day." I told her I would stay home and we would wait until she thought it was time, and then we could calmly drive to the local hospital.

Everything was going according to plan, until, out of the blue, she said, "J.T., I want my regular obstetrician in Sarasota."

I was dumbfounded. She was a Registered Nurse. She had run the obstetrics floor at Mercy Hospital when we lived in Miami. The baby was on its way.

While I stuttered, she said, "You have that plane and you fly it any place you want to go. I want you to fly me to Sarasota."

My wife is a gentle person who seldom asks for anything out of the ordinary. She always allows me to do any hair-brained thing I want to. But about this request, there was no doubt she was serious.

Although it seemed crazy, I considered the possibility. If we took off, we would be within twenty minutes maximum of a hospital, provided ambulances were on standby along the flight path. I asked her, "If I can put it together, do you really want to do this?"

She didn't hesitate. In her usual soft voice she said, "Yes."

I called flight control and explained the situation. They said that is what they were there for. They would do anything to assist us. (Things are different now.) I called the local field where we hangared *The Gnat* and asked them to roll it out, fuel it, and remove the stick on the passenger side to accommodate Pat's condition.

We were off the ground in ten minutes. Our first hospital was Brooksville, and the point of no return from Leesburg was seventeen miles. After that, we were committed to Brooksville. After Brooksville, the point of no return was Tampa, twenty-two miles farther. The flight controllers welcomed us into each segment and bid us a pleasant day and good luck, then turned us over to the controller in the next segment.

The ambulances were on standby and passed their good wishes to us through the controllers. There was constant dialogue on the radio about our status, and some suggestions for a name. It was old Florida at its best. When we cleared the Tampa point of no return, Sarasota approach control informed us they had a taxi on the ramp, anticipating our arrival.

A National Air Line flight relinquished priority to us in landing order. We landed and rolled to a stop. The ground crew said they would tie down the Luscombe. We had a pleasant ride past Ringling Art School, past the house where I asked Pat to marry me, and on to Sarasota Memorial Hospital.

Our daughter was born an hour and a half later. I called flight control. They said they were glad to be of service and would pass the good news back up the line.

Florida has always been a wonderful place to live and raise a family. It also has friendly skies.

Chapter 11

DOUBLEWIDES

I often wonder how or why one can stray from his or her limited area of expertise and go sailing off into uncharted waters, firmly believing they are making a wise decision, and feeling virtuous at the same time.

In 1953, I did exactly that. We were building a house in Sarasota in the late summer. The heat was unbearable. Maybe it affected my brain. All manufacturing was done indoors in the shade, which led me to the conviction that all homes should be built on assembly lines. Yes, it would be simple; they could be built in two halves in a factory, and joined together on the site. After a minimum of consideration, I concluded it not only could be done, but I could do it.

There is nothing wrong with a daydream. The danger lies in becoming obsessed with one's dreams. And I did.

Crackers like me never make a long story short; they make a short story long. But I will try to be brief because Lucille will pester me if I am not.

In Tampa, I built a model, and raised the capital to build a factory in Leesburg, Florida. It was not really that simple. I promised the investors that I would build the factory, as well as produce sufficient houses to impress a large corporation of the marketability of our modular homes, all within a year. We would then spin it off, as they say in investment firms; sell the concept and factory at a profit. I ignored the fact that I was an artist and designer, not a manufacturer.

With the capital in hand, there was nothing left to do but cast off. I bought a perfectly good cow pasture in Leesburg and turned it into a factory, with the help of thirty unskilled workers and two semiskilled carpenters. There were some problems, especially on Monday mornings. The sheriff routinely rounded up several of my youthful workers and charged them for overreacting to misunderstandings that had occurred on the previous Saturday night. Usually, after solemn promises to be model citizens committed to nonviolence, he would release the ones who had not made the same promise the preceding week. That, however, was not the case when one was hauled off to jail for imitating a flasher on the local U.S. Highway.

We finished the factory (the world's cheapest pole building), and the first production house rolled off the

line. But there was a problem. The banks would not finance the houses unless the loans were guaranteed by the Federal Housing Administration, commonly referred to as the FHA. This opened a whole new ball game. Local authorities said that because our construction methods were unconventional, I would have to get them approved in the FHA offices in Washington.

Lucille reminded me of the fact that I had never previously undertaken any of the things involved in my current task, so I figured I might as well go to Washington and get the approval myself. What the hell—in for a penny, in for a pound.

Being naive in matters pertaining to government was an understatement. Nevertheless, I caught a flight from Orlando to Washington on an old Eastern gas engine DC-7. Thankfully, it was before the beginning of the jet age, so passengers had six to seven hours to think about the stability of their businesses and stomachs, while four, four-blade propellers augured through one cold front after another. After a lot of thinking, I found no solutions. Lucille was no help. She only trusted flying on her own power.

The flight arrived at Washington National in the beginning of a snowstorm. It was my first time in the nation's capital, and I didn't know the Washington Monument from the capital, and I most certainly didn't know where the Federal Housing Administration was. The only address I did have was the address of a law firm that one of my lawyer friends gave me. He said I could go there and his friend would let me use one of his secretaries to type any reports or documents I needed.

I caught a cab to the Willard Hotel, one that a stewardess had suggested. It didn't matter to me that the historical old hotel was in need of restoration. In fact, I didn't know it was historic. I checked in, consumed with the business at hand. A quick look out of my room's window revealed Pennsylvania Avenue and a small corner of the U.S. Capitol. The snow was coming down harder. Florida Crackers normally go into a state of hyper-giddiness when they see snow, but for me this was not the time or place. Most of the night was spent planning strategies. None were any good, so I elected to just go to the F.H.A. offices to see what would happen. After breakfast, I grabbed a taxi to the Federal Housing Administration's national headquarters, just off K Street. It was imposing, especially to a Cracker from Cross Creek. Inside, the foyer gleamed with highly polished terrazzo floors, complementing the marble fascias around a bank of six elevators. The doors were stainless steel with the great seal of the F.H.A. emblazoned on each door in bronze and blue.

The building directory, sealed under plate glass, looked like an honor role of powerful executives. I followed the titles and down near the bottom was the Director of Codes and Enforcement. He had a name I couldn't pronounce, but thought his receptionist would help me with that. The uniformed elevator operator herded me, along with a number of men all dressed in three-piece suits, into the third elevator. I managed to squeeze from the back to the front in time to get off on the fourth floor where, maybe, the office of the director of "new problems" would be waiting to accommodate my humble needs. The receptionist finished storing her makeup in a side drawer of her desk. Without looking up, she asked, totally detached, "Can I help you?" "Yes. I'm from Florida and need a clearance for some modest changes in the inspection procedures for modular housing." "Do you have an appointment?" she asked, still not looking up.

I said, "No, but I would be willing to wait." No response. "Possibly you could direct me to the person who could help me?" She looked at a list Scotch taped to a panel extending from her desk. She retrieved her makeup case back from the drawer and mumbled, "Perhaps you should go to Administration on the third floor." I left without seeing her face, feeling confident I hadn't missed anything.

I retreated to the lobby and out to a little triangle-shaped public park. A small bronze plaque stated that the great statesman and philosopher, Bernard Baruch, had used the little park as a place to relax and commiserate with his fellow men. My friend back at Cross Creek, Bernie Bass, had said Bernard Baruch was the smartest man in the world, so I sat down for some Baruch bench thinking. Lucille, I need a plan, a plan that can be implemented. Soon! Bernie, who read *National Geographic* from cover to cover, had formulated definite opinions on matters relative to government and its elected officials. He believed they would sincerely like to help people if it didn't cost them any prestige or votes. In addition, they would avoid anything that would require more than a few minutes of their staff's time, plus they insisted on assurance that they could take credit if a project or proposal went well.

My doublewide houses, built under conventional house codes, would be a good thing for housing in this country. Therefore, every Congressman should want the method of inspection amended to allow them to be manufactured.

Sitting there on a bench where the great Bernard Baruch had sat on (until this day I do not know why he was famous), I had thoughts of great world consequence. I decided that I needed to simplify my request. It needed a simple name. No matter that it did not have a clear meaning, as long as it sounded routine and official. "Structural variance" had possibilities, but didn't have the right ring. Then Lucille, or Bernard Baruch's bench, gave me a perfect one, a "bulletin." That was it. It was vague enough and still sounded official. From that moment on, I was in Washington to get a "bulletin," and come hell or high water, I was going to get one.

I remembered back at the county seat, when Congressmen were running for office, how they elaborated on the hard work they did, tending to their constituents' business. "If you reelect me, and you ever have a problem, write me a letter, or better, you come to Washington and I will personally see that it is solved to your satisfaction."

I thought, I am a citizen and I am going to take them up on their offer. I am going to Congress and get Congress to persuade F.H.A. to give me the necessary papers. Unfortunately, civics was not one of the bright spots in my formal education. I knew there were two Houses, but was not clear as to exactly what their functions were. No matter, I would solicit help from both.

I spent the evening planning what I would say if they agreed to listen. An urge to think of the consequence of failure tried constantly to creep into my mind, but to my surprise, Lucille was there, scolding and admonishing them away. I found myself enjoying her company, and grateful for the intervention.

Unaware that I should have letters of introduction and powerful references, I charged up Capitol Hill. Wearing my only dark three-piece suit, and carrying a black briefcase seemed appropriate. (I later discovered I looked more like a member of the Japanese trade delegation.) Giving myself more time to think, I walked down Pennsylvania Avenue to the Capitol Building. I had a plan, and even though it might be hokey, it was better than going from receptionist to receptionist in the Federal Housing Administration. Soliciting the individual Congressmen to monitor my progress, or the lack of progress, on a daily basis, seemed plausible. If they knew I was being ignored or given the run-around, they might be motivated to intercede on my behalf. It was worth a try. Bernie just might be right.

A man shoveling remnants of snow from the sidewalk was kind enough to point out the Senate offices in the wing across from Union Station, and the Congressional offices at the opposite end of that magnificent Capitol Building. I climbed the steps and entered the Senate wing. The first door on the right was designated, in modest-sized gold leaf, "Senator Richard Russell of Georgia." My mother and dad were from Georgia. What better place to start than with Senator Russell?

I went in and asked a lady with an Atlanta accent if I could speak to the Senator, assuring her I would take no more than two minutes, thirty seconds of his time. She stepped behind the partition and returned momentarily with a gentleman whose soft-spoken manner made him seem like the floor manager of an elite fifth avenue jeweler. "I am Senator Russell's Administrative Assistant."

I introduced myself. "I am J. T. I have come from Florida, and if you will hear me out, I promise it will take only two minutes and thirty seconds of your time."

He said, "How can you be so precise?"

I answered, "Because I practiced and timed what I needed to say before coming here."

He laughed. "Being brief is an unusual occurrence in Washington, and most refreshing." He looked at his watch and said, "Begin."

Without hesitation, I launched into my rehearsed speech. "I am sure your office can be of great help to me and the people across the country. Senator

Russell did the country a great service when he supported and voted for the establishment of the Federal Housing Administration. (I wasn't sure that he did, but didn't expect him to deny it since it was a popular success.) It does provide finance for the millions of Americans who otherwise could not obtain it. It was also good that Congress insisted on codes for construction that insure the homes will be of high standards and will last the lifetime of the homeowner's. "However, there is one flaw. The codes and standards cause the cost of construction to exceed the amount that low-income families can afford. Low-income families are the ones who need these houses the most."

The Administrator started to speak.

"I have a minute and fifty eight seconds left."

He smiled and said, "Sorry."

I began again. "Down in Florida, we have addressed the problem, and concluded that it would be wrong to compromise the codes, and therefore the only way we can reduce the cost and meet the codes is to put the houses on an assembly line similar to the way the automotive industry provided an affordable car for the average American family." I reiterated the virtues of modular housing. In addition, I told him I believed the Housing Administration would eventually give me a deviation of their rules, to change their inspections from the field to our factory. I pointed out that we had been advised not to ask until we had the factory on line. We had accomplished that, and the immediate problem was that we could not wait weeks, and perhaps months, because the cost of waiting could cause us to eventually have to abandon the entire plan.

I caught a needed breath. "What I have come to Washington for is to ask F.H.A. to make those inspections in the factory. We will pay for an inspector, or they can do periodic inspections, with a heavy penalty for any violations of their codes." I felt like a Jehovah's Witness that had knocked on a door while the occupant was taking a bath. Nevertheless, I plowed ahead and noticed several staff members were listening. "I am not here to ask the Senator for anything at this time. I am sure the people down at Federal Housing will give me a hearing, and eventually grant our request. What I propose to do is send you a daily report of my progress, and in the event I should run into any problem, you will be aware of the total situation and might intercede on my behalf. In a benedictory tone, I said, "Thank you and Senator Russell for your time. With your permission, I will send you my daily report starting tomorrow."

Senator Russell's administrative assistant said, "There is no hurry, Mr. Glisson. It sounds like a promising advance for housing, and I am sure the Senator will be interested in your progress."

Lucille said, "Don't stop to talk. Leave now, while you are ahead."

I was delighted with myself. I visited ten more Senate offices using the same format. They were all courteous to me and promised to follow my progress. My only criterion for congressional selection was names from states east of Texas and south of New Jersey. I had lunch in the Capitol and went to the congressional wing after lunch. Congressman Billy Matthews, originally from Hawthorne (the little town where I went to public school), treated me as if I were a long lost friend and thoroughly acquainted himself with my project.

He said in his diplomatic Southern accent, "Mr. Glisson, I am truly grateful that you came to me." He gave me his number and insisted that I call if I needed any help.

When the offices closed at the end of the day, I had eleven supporters at the Capitol. The following day, I picked up seven more. I decided it was time for me to go back to the Federal Housing Administration and ask for my "bulletin."

Thursday morning, I was back at the F.H.A., being maneuvered from one department to another. I asked for appointments with anyone above receptionists. They referred me to the offices that referred me to the same offices to which I had initially been referred. Most everyone was cordial and polite, until I asked for something or someone specifically.

At the end of the day, I was exhausted and batting zero. It was harder than running from the game wardens. At five o'clock, I walked the few blocks to the law firm on K Street, met my lawyer friend's friend, and asked if I could get a secretary to type reports for me. He was friendly and wanted to help. The secretary he suggested I use was what I later came to recognize as a typical Washington law firm secretary. She spoke without looking directly at me. (Therefore she could honestly testify that she had never seen me.) At the same time, she was pleasant, efficient, and seemed eager to help. I dictated my day's activities at the offices of the Federal Housing Administration, and tried to be factual, avoiding any personal criticism or sarcasm. Nevertheless, the report was a scenario of the bureaucratic run-around at its finest. In two days I contacted twenty-three, Senators and Congressmen, soliciting their support. My newly acquired secretarial assistant ran off twenty-three daily reports and mailed them to each one daily.

Friday morning in the coffee shop, I met two lobbyists. They asked why I was in Washington. I told them I was there to get a change in the inspection procedures at the F.H.A. They wanted to know if I had rented an apartment, assuming that I was prepared to stay for a year or more. I told them I had to get the change made by Friday of the coming week. They broke into uncontrolled laughter. "Surely you're joking." They wished me luck with the same enthusiasm they would have had if I had told them that I planned to win the lottery three weeks in succession.

In the offices, everyone was talking about St. Patrick's Day coming up the following Tuesday. The holiday seemed terribly important to the personnel at the F.H.A. At Cross Creek, we probably would have never heard of Ireland's patron saint if it hadn't been for his reported power to purge snakes from an entire country. Trying to be as subtle as possible, I asked why the occasion was so important to people whose names were Sanchez, Baudine, and Steinburg.

The general consensus seemed to be that St. Patrick's birthday was the last official drinking holiday until Oktoberfest.

I wandered into the Office of Architectural Standards where their plans for the Saint's birthday were being discussed. The enthusiasm was contagious. I found myself talking with the Director of that section, who told me to call him Bill. He told an Irish joke, and I countered with a Cracker joke, converted to Irish doing a pathetic imitation of Barry Fitzgerald. The joke, to my surprise, was a knee slapper.

The Director asked me where I was from. I told him Leesburg, Florida. He was a sports fisherman and was curious about bass fishing. We discussed it briefly before he had to excuse himself, citing a busy schedule. Before he left, he said, "Some of us get together after five in the pub next door for a beer. Why don't you join us? That is, if you don't have conflicting appointments."

My first thought was I would cancel an appointment with St. Patrick himself before I would miss being there.

Lucille whispered, "Shame."

At seven minutes after five, which seemed an appropriate time, I entered the pub. The atmosphere was loud. Some of the patrons were singing Irish songs, while others were engaged in conversations with individuals who were five tables across the room. The Director of Architectural Standards motioned me to join him and his four friends at their corner table. He introduced me. "This is Glisson from Florida, who is in town to get a bulletin." No one asked what a bulletin was or for what.

Bill's friends all told Irish jokes while consuming beer and ale. I thoroughly enjoyed the evening, and introduced them to Cracker stories on the premise that Crackers had sufficient Irish blood for any occasion. There were songs about Killarney, Galloway Bay, and especially, Mrs. Murphy's Chowder. Then at eight o'clock, the party abruptly ended and all the participants scurried home for the weekend.

I walked over to the law office on K Street and dictated my report to Marilyn, the stenographer. I reported that I had been unable to speak to anyone who could consider my request for the change in inspection procedures. Even though I had some official appointments, they resulted in meetings with individuals with no authority to be of any help. I reported the hospitality I received from the Office of Architectural Standards and its Director. I ended the report optimistically, with the assumption that surely I would find the proper person who would issue my "bulletin" on Monday.

The weekend was not a total loss. I spent Saturday in the Corcoran Museum of Art. Normally, it would have been paradise, but I was plagued by thoughts of the clock running, and the mounting probability of returning to Florida without my "bulletin."

Sunday, I went to the National Archives, saw the Declaration of Independence, the Constitution and the flag that inspired Francis Scott Key. When I got back to the Willard, I was overwhelmed with patriotism.

Monday and Tuesday were an abrupt return to reality. Although I had become a familiar figure around the offices, no one knew how to help me. Amazingly, no one asked what a "bulletin" was. I was even given an appointment with the Manager of Building Maintenance. I became convinced that the staff of the F.H.A. had majored in evasion. There were some that most certainly had master's degrees in that subject, and possibly some in the upper echelon with PhDs in the College of Citizenry Evasion.

In nine days, all I had accomplished was attaining the status of being a harmless source of entertainment. My new friend, the Director of Architectural Standards, told me he would be glad to draw up a bulletin if it were approved by the proper authorities. He, of course, did not know specifically from whom I could get that approval.

I met with the fellows in the pub each night, and then went to the office on K Street and had Marilyn do my report to the Congressmen. We listed several individuals each day with whom I had appointments, that were sorry they couldn't be of any help. Lucille had only one suggestion: I should buy flowers and give them to Marilyn who typed an extra hour each night. And I did.

Wednesday, it was obvious that I had to start closing the gap if I hoped to get my bulletin and return home by Friday. I deliberately psyched myself up over breakfast, and charged into the F.H.A. building determined to give it a last try before falling back on Congress. I told everyone that my partners were convinced that I was being given the run-around, and that they were on the verge of chartering a plane and coming to Washington to see what the hold-up was. This would have been entirely true if they, my partners, knew about my progress in Washington (or lack of it), and how fragile their investment was without the bulletin.

I moved from fourth level to third level shortly before lunch. Three executives, who had gathered around the water cooler, suggested I return to Florida and re-document the entire project, and then submit it to a quarterly planning conference that was coming up.

I yelled, "This is a crisis! If I don't see someone of high authority, my entire organization is going to descend on Washington within hours." They became sympathetic to my cause, and arranged an appointment with the Housing Administration's number two man, the Assistant Director of the Federal Housing Administration, for 4:45 that afternoon.

The Assistant Director was cordial, polite, and condescending. He had his receptionist serve me coffee in porcelain china. After a polite introduction, he asked, "Where are you from, Mr. Glisson?" I told him. He said central Florida had always been of special interest to him. I tried to introduce the concept of modular housing and our need for a variance in inspection. He politely side-stepped my effort, and wanted to know about the effect of population growth in Florida. Then he told me a lengthy story that he concluded with, "It has been a privilege meeting you Mr., uh, Glisson. I will pass along your request. It is five o'clock and my transportation is waiting." He then started for a side door.

I said as forcefully as I could without shouting, "Mr. Mason, you did not give me an opportunity to tell you why I came to Washington, and specifically to the Federal Housing Administration. My partners have spent a great deal of their money, and I have seventy-five employees who will not have jobs if you do not do something to clear the barrier that is keeping us from providing the very product this agency was created to institute."

He was annoyed, but maintained his senior executive decorum. "Mr. Glisson, I am sympathetic with your problems. You come back in the morning." He went through a side door and closed it behind him.

When I dictated my report, I felt that it would be a mistake to express my pessimism. After all, Mr. Mason had told me to come back. So, I reported a cordial meeting with the Assistant Administrator, but covered our meeting in detail. Giving him the benefit of doubt, I disclosed that I was confident he would take the situation in hand and push my request through first thing Thursday morning.

My newfound stenographer friend was outraged. She said, "That jerk has no intention of helping you."

Lucille said, "Relax."

I didn't relax and I didn't sleep much. Thursday morning on Bernard Baruch's bench, I waited for the F.H.A. building to open for what I hoped would be an appointment with the Assistant Director. At 9:30, I entered his office. The receptionist acted as if she was waiting for me. She looked at a blank note pad and said, "Good morning, Mr. Glisson. I have a message for you. The director is away on annual leave. He said he is so sorry, but in the haste of the moment yesterday afternoon, he forgot about his leave. However, he feels you will have no problem if you pursue your request at the proper levels."

I was not surprised. I took the stairs down to the lobby because they were faster. Then I stalked out of the building and caught a cab to the Senate wing of the Capitol. In the taxi, I reveled in a deliberate state of indignant outrage.

I entered Senator Russell's office with a chip on both shoulders. I asked to see the Senator's Administrative Assistant. He came out to the reception desk immediately. I told him I had come to Washington in good faith, and I had been dumb enough to believe my government would try to help me, or any citizen who had a legitimate need for service.

He interrupted me and said, "The Senator would like to see you, if you will come with me." He led me into a luxurious but comfortable office.

Senator Russell came around his desk with his hand extended. "Mr. Glisson, we have followed your, I should say, lack of progress with concern, and I have to admit a certain amount of amusement. Your daily reports are indeed satiric, but unfortunately, a true pathetic statement of some of Washington's concern for the citizenry."

I blurted out, "The Assistant Director of the F.H.A. promised to help me today and now his secretary tells me he forgot he is indefinitely out on annual leave."

The distinguished old Senator (he appeared old to me when I was thirty-three) asked me to have a seat, and then in his soft Georgia accent, asked his secretary if she would get him Mr. Robert Weaver, Director of Federal Housing.

A moment later, he said, "Good morning, sir. This is Richard Russell. I have a man here in my office that has caused me to question whether we here in Washington are capable or worthy of serving the people of this country. Mr. Glisson is a fine young man whose family is from my state. He came here two weeks ago to ask your agency for what appears to be a simple request. He has given my office a daily report of his progress in your offices, and they appear to represent a total lack of responsibility and concern by your staff." There was a short pause. Then the Senator continued, "I have supported the funding of the F.H.A. from its inception, and I recall your statements about the necessity for flexibility in providing finance for housing across the country."

There was another pause. Then Senator Russell spoke again. "His name is J. T. Glisson. He is with Finest Manufacturing Company in Leesburg, Florida." There was another pause and then, "Thank you. We will follow your progress." Senator Russell put down the phone and told me, "Mr. Glisson, I believe you will be successful down at Federal Housing, and I hope you feel free to stop by this office whenever you are in Washington." I promised him a report and thanked him and his staff.

Out in the hall, when I was sure no one was looking, I did my version of the Irish jig, then headed for the next Senator's office. The scenario was generally the same. They had all apparently read my reports with great humor, and discussed the adventures of the Florida Cracker lost in the Washington bureaucratic maze. Most of them called the Director of the F.H.A. Two called the Cabinet Member who presided over the agency.

When the clocks throughout the capital struck, five o'clock, I had touched base with fourteen of the eighteen Congressmen I had originally contacted. Congressman Billy Matthews sent his Administrative Assistant to personally contact the officials at the F.H.A. I have never been more tired and pleased than I was when I arrived back at the Willard. Lucille was pleased with herself as well.

Behind the hotel desk, my call box looked like a miniature landfill stuffed with yellow, white, and pink messages, all from the Federal Housing Administration. The first one came just after I talked to Senator Russell. Another had come from the Assistant Director at 3:30. The first messages were demanding. "Come to this office immediately," and, "It is imperative you come to my office as soon as possible." They became more polite as the day progressed. I went downstairs for dinner.

Friday morning, when I entered the lobby, the starter for the elevators met me and asked, "Are you Glisson?"

I answered, "Yes."

He said, "Would you follow me?"

He led me into an elevator that was on hold, and the two of us zipped up to the top floor, then down a wide hall into an office that had "Robert C. Weaver - Director - Federal Housing Administration - United States of America" printed in gold leaf on an ornate oak wood door. The office was auspicious and unusually large. A massive mahogany desk sat centered in the end of the room, flanked by an American flag adorned with a gold eagle positioned at the top of a polished staff. A large conference table was to my right and an informal lounge to the left.

A tall imposing man, behind the desk, rose as we entered the room.

The elevator operator said, "This is Mr. Glisson."

The man behind the desk thanked him, stood, leaned forward, placed both hands flat on his desk, looked directly into my eyes, and said, "It is indeed a privilege to meet you, Mr. Glisson. What can I do for you?" I started into my explanation of how we had come to design and manufacture the doublewide modular house. He held up his hand and in a soft controlled voice said, "No explanation is necessary. What can we do for you, here in this office, at this moment?"

I said, "I have to have my bulletin, the one I came to Washington for."

He pushed a button and spoke in a condescending tone to the intercom, "Would you have the two staff members I spoke to you about come into my office? Thank you." He motioned me to have a seat in the lounge area. I declined as politely as possible. The Assistant Director that was away on annual leave, and the Director of Architectural Standards came through the door together. The Assistant Director looked at me as if I stolen his golf clubs and wrecked his limousine. The young man from Architectural Standards spoke to me with an expression of "damned if it ain't the Cracker Irishman!" I think he would have laughed if the Director hadn't been there. Bill was a nice guy that had to work within the system.

The Director said, "Gentlemen, how long will it take to get the bulletin that Mr. Glisson is here for?"

His assistant answered, "There will be some problems to iron out, but we . . ."

Director Weaver interrupted, "No. I want to know, with all priorities set aside, how long it will take to type or print the thing and have it in Mr. Glisson's hand."

Andrews said, "Sir, with it cleared by you, I can have it done in two hours."

The Director spoke with absolute authority, "Then do it." He returned to his soft voice. "Mr. Glisson has been detained far longer than I would have preferred." He looked directly at his Assistant Director. "Sir, would you arrange transportation for Mr. Glisson to his hotel and the airport in exactly two hours?" He glanced at his watch. "He needs to be on his way. I understand they are doing great things in Florida." He turned to me and said, "I hope you every success with your houses, and please extend my best wishes to your colleagues and your many friends down on the Hill."

Lucille and I boarded the plane with the bulletin in hand. Stealing a Winston Churchill line, I told Lucille, "I believe this is Washington's and our finest hour." And to an extent, I still do. However, when I reflect back on the hunt and final capture of the "bulletin," I have to give Lucille the credit. I couldn't have done it without her.

We ran the factory for a year, producing two or three houses a week. Most were financed by the F.H.A. We sold the majority of the houses in Florida, but some were shipped across the country and into Canada. Two were shipped to the Middle East.

All was not easy after we got the "bulletin." On one occasion, I contracted to put one of the houses in the National Home Show in Chicago's McCormick Place. It seemed simple enough, until one of our drivers reached the edge of town and refused to pull it in Chicago traffic. The fee for the show had been paid in advance, and there was no way we would miss the show. I told the driver pulling the other half to wait, I would come and pull it myself.

Another long story short—In the loop, there was a street that ran under Chicago's main post office. I started under, and promptly got the half house jammed beneath the post office and the street. Every ill-tempered cop in Chicago showed up immediately. Traffic backed up. Everyone shouted and waved their arms. Everyone in the loop blew their horns and cursed a lot. The other driver, fortunately, had experienced a low underpass before. He ordered fifty 18' X 2" X 8" pieces of wood, and jacked up the side where the roof sloped down, thus lowering the high side. Then he made a higher track for the wheel on the low side to run on. It only took five hours to free the house and the Chicago post office. On the bright side, there were so many policemen there that everyone thought someone else gave us the ticket.

I promised my partners, when they funded the venture, that we would spin off the business in a year, and we did. Chance Vought Aircraft purchased the company in '61. We didn't make any money, but we brought doublewide homes into the American market. Today, there are more than two million modular homes (doublewides), all very similar to the first one that came off the assembly line in Leesburg. And the last time I checked, there had been hundreds of bulletins issued by the Federal Housing Administration.

The F.H.A. was up-graded to the Department of Housing and Urban Development during Lyndon Johnson's presidency. Director Robert Weaver became Secretary Weaver, and incidentally, the first black Cabinet Member in our history. He was truly a man who knew how to get things done.

This is still a great country. We have some great leaders. The last time (also the only time) I needed its support, the Congress came through with flying colors.

Chapter 12

MIAMI TO YEEHAW

When pilots talk about flying, they generally tell about their wildest experiences, like the times when weather or mechanical failure put them in impossible situations requiring great skill and daring. They neglect to tell their listeners of the hundreds of hours they have spent savoring the sheer beauty of the rising and setting of the sun, of billowing clouds, or an occasional rainbow that formed a perfect circle called a pilot's halo. Pilots are reluctant to admit that, up there, they really are different; that they share an affection with their craft similar to a cowboy's relation with his horse; and that they are more philosophical, impartial, and spiritual when they are in that special world that begins only a few hundred feet above the ground.

I have several hundred hours of flying time, and I have tried to honor Boots' first and last rules of flying, "When you got a problem, put it on the ground." However, there have been times when things got complicated and necessitated some additional rules. One of those times occurred in south Florida in the early 'sixties.

Back then, there were few regulations in the uncrowded skies. Pilots were pretty much on their own, unless they were in a heavy traffic area or could endanger someone other than themselves. It was not necessary to file a flight plan and you could fly into most airports without a radio. All you had to do was approach the field at a forty-five degree angle and waggle the wings. The tower would give you a green light, indicating you were free to land. Occasionally, they gave you an orange light that indicated there was traffic and that you should hold in the pattern around the field. A red light was an order to clear the pattern, but that was given only when they had extremely hazardous conditions.

In Florida, there are thunderstorms about eighty per cent of the time. The Luscombe was small and slow, but if you could stay in it, the wings would stay on it. Not unlike real mules, it was stubborn and required a positive hand, but more importantly, it was strong and dependable.

I have always believed the worst pilots in America were Florida pilots. At least they were back when I was young. In Florida, there are no rocks in the clouds like there are in the Appalachian and Rocky Mountain states. And if you were between the Gulf and the Atlantic, you considered yourself on course. As long as you cleared the radio towers, you didn't have to worry about altitude, and you could always see the Gulf or Atlantic coast, eliminating the need for navigational skills. When weather conditions were bad, pilots were supposed to convert from Visual Flight Rules (VFR) to Instrument Flight Rules (IFR), and to navigate by instruments. Most private planes didn't have navigational instruments, so when they flew in marginal conditions, they defined IFR as "I Follow Railroads."

I believe Lucille got her full-time assignment with me the day I soloed. I don't have any idea how angels are selected, but I suspect she did it as an act of altruism. She let me know loud and clear that if one needed a motor to fly, one should stay on the ground. In addition, I did not endear myself to her with my eagerness to ignore my lack of experience. I believe my guardian angel Lucille originated the expression, "There are old pilots, and there are bold pilots, but there are no old, bold pilots." She never tired of repeating that phrase.

My company had men scattered all over the state, assembling the doublewide houses, with one or two men processing paperwork in the field. It occurred to me that with the Luscombe, I could do the paperwork and payrolls in two days. Prior to that, it required two men, driving company cars five and sometimes six days a week. Naturally, I didn't mind flying around if it benefited the company. We had competent managers at the factory.

The task proved to be more difficult than I expected. There were no airstrips in places like Myakka City, Fort Lonesome, and Holopaw. Places like Arcadia and Clermont often had two inches of water standing in un-mowed grass. The best landing spots were maintained by the county and state road departments. It was rare to fly a straight line from one point to another. Thunderstorms necessitated constant weaving, and occasionally a compromised destination. There is nothing in this state I respect more than a healthy thunderhead.

I often recalled Boots' first and last rules. He referred to thunderstorms as mule killers. It was frequently necessary to go in and out of old Imison Airport in Jacksonville, Tampa International, and Orlando's Herndon Airport, wagging the wings and holding for a green light.

My radio was weak, and the Luscombe didn't have landing lights. On one occasion, a Tampa controller offered to buy me some brighter bulbs for my navigation lights. I loved flying, and was lucky to have flown at a time when there was so much freedom in the skies. There was little or no traffic in outlying areas, especially at lower altitudes.

One particular late afternoon, I found myself in Ft. Pierce. I had zig-zagged back and forth across the state for two days, landing in cow pastures and roadways, picking up finance documents and construction permits. It was "Thank

God, It's Friday" time, near sundown. On an impulse, I thought it would be a good time to visit an old friend in Ft. Lauderdale. I could fly down, my friend and I could go to dinner, and I would fly back to Leesburg on Saturday morning.

It was on one of those infrequent flights when I was flying in absolute accord with Lucille, Captain Eddy Rickenbacker, General Hap Arnold and all the CAA's rules, that things got out of hand. (The Civil Aviation Authority, CAA., later became the FAA, the Federal Aviation Authority.) Of course, Lucille reminded me that the southeastern coast was unusually congested, and in addition, the Cuban missile crisis had south Florida on military alert. The situation could boil over at any moment. I told her I didn't expect Castro to invade south Florida, and that I was unequivocally competent to fly in south Florida traffic.

I took off in *The Gnat*, and filed an en-route flight plan to Ft. Lauderdale. It was the first flight plan I had filed in several months.

In the air, I marveled at the beauty of the southeastern coast. The moon was coming up over the Atlantic, and the twinkling lights of the small towns strung along U.S. Highway 1 were like a lighted runway to Lauderdale. A half-hour later, I passed over Palm Beach at fifteen hundred feet. The elegant old Breakers Hotel, tastefully lighted and bathed in moonlight, was a clear landmark. It was one of those times and places when it is inconceivable not to savor the privilege of flying. There is no place on this planet as peaceful as a solo flight on a moonlit night in perfect weather.

I passed over the old Pompano Marine Air Base within seconds of my estimated time of arrival, and called Lauderdale approach control, informing them One Eight Kilo was approaching their field. A casual controller came back, "One Eight Kilo, we do not have any traffic in the area, and suggest you continue your present heading south. When you are east of the field, give us a call and we will clear you to land." I thought General Hap Arnold (Chief of Staff, U.S. Army Air Corps during W.W. II) would be proud to be riding right hand seat with me. There could be no doubt I still had it. Lucille reminded me of the Navy planes that took off from Opalocka, never to be heard from again, attesting to the Bermuda Triangle theory for those who believed in that sort of thing.

Every pilot that has logged more than forty hours knows that it is hard to find an airport in a city at night. Airports are dark areas, and at that time, Lauderdale Airport adjoined the Florida Everglades. I was familiar with the area, but I couldn't spot the airport. I called the tower and said I was having a problem spotting the field. They answered that I was still north of the field and should continue south.

The Luscombe was slow, but one cannot fly in one direction over Lauderdale for more than a few minutes, without overflying it. The tower called back and advised that they were picking up some commercial traffic and wanted to know my location. I told them it was three minutes south of the location when we last transmitted. All I could see on the ground were neon Budweiser signs in bar windows, and streetlights.

The tower came back with a tone of urgency. "One Eight Kilo, do you see a field to the south-southwest?"

I said, "There is one, but I think it is too far to be your field. I suggest I do a one-eighty and go back and pick up an approach further to the west."

He said, "The field you have in sight is Lauderdale. We have you in sight. Proceed directly to the field. You are clear to land."

I pushed the throttle forward on a course directly to the airport we had identified. When I let down on a direct approach, I immediately lost radio contact with the tower. I lined up on a strip and proceeded to land.

The field did not look like the Lauderdale Airport. The area had grown during the ten years since I lived in south Florida. But I was committed.

A hundred feet off, I saw a line of monstrous commercial airliners on final approach, stretching to the western horizon. Our flight paths would intersect at the center of the field. Their landing speed was faster than my top speed. I did a dogleg, and put the mule down on a taxi way in the northwest corner of the field.

I was confused. The airport was a different configuration than any I had seen in south Florida. I wondered if it could be the Air Force Base near Homestead, but that was certainly too far south. Maybe they had built a new Lauderdale Airport, further out of town.

A tanker truck was unloading into an underground storage tank when I came to a stop. I taxied over to the truck with the door open and shouted, "What's the name of this field?"

I heard his reply loud and clear: "Miami International."

I have never felt so stupid and angry in my life. Someone had screwed up, and I didn't think it was me. There was one thing I was sure of; I wasn't about to try to fly out in all that traffic. I cut across the field, toward a line of four-engine DC-6's and Constellations parked along side a huge terminal.

No one has ever been more unwelcome than me and my Luscombe, *Gnat*. The ground crews for American, Braniff, Varig, and Aerolinas were waving me off like I had a cargo of *E-coli* bacterium. I decided I was going to park. They could fight over who impounded my plane and who got my license. I taxied up under the wing of a Delta DC-6 and chopped the throttle.

Everyone out on the tarmac stared at me like I was the first Martian they had ever seen. Thankfully, I couldn't hear what they were saying because planes were warming up and taxiing all over the place. I went in the first door I found. It was the Delta pilot's lounge. Ten or twelve pilots, all in uniform, were shooting the breeze, or reading. Before anyone could ask why I was there, I asked, "Is there a phone here? I want to call the tower or your flight control."

They looked puzzled. One said, "Use that one over there on the wall. Just pick it up and tell them who you want."

A voice answered and I said, "I want to talk to the tower."

Every one in the room was suddenly quiet. A voice answered, "Tower."

I replied, "I am on your field. I flew in here because of a mistake."

"You are on this field?"

"Yes."

"Where are you now and where did you come from?"

"I am J.T. Glisson, my home base is Leesburg, and I am in what looks like the Delta pilots' ready room."

"You are here on Miami International?"

"I just told you, yes."

"You landed a plane here on this field without clearance?"

"I was cleared to land by the Ft. Lauderdale tower."

"This is not Ft. Lauderdale,"

Every pilot in the room gathered around me, stifling their laughter.

"Yes, I know this is not Lauderdale. That is why I am calling you."

"Where is your plane now?"

"It is just outside, parked beneath the wing of a Delta DC-6."

"Will you hold for a minute?"

"Yes."

I could hear other voices in the background. A different person came on the line.

"What type of aircraft are you flying?"

"A Luscombe."

"Say again."

"A Luscombe."

"Please hold."

I could hear a discussion that lasted until someone said it was a very small, antiquated private aircraft. The tower came back, sounding somewhere between distraught and confused.

"Will you continue to hold?"

While I waited, all the pilots wanted to know what happened and I tried to explain. One senior officer, with gold strips half way to his elbow, told me that they had moved the terminal from the north side of the field to the east side, three years back. No wonder I was confused. They all seemed to think it was hilarious. They agreed that I had set off a panic among the usually calm, collected controllers.

Two or three minutes later the tower came back.

"Sir, have you used your transmitter to contact Miami?"

I said, "No. I was transmitting to Lauderdale until I was too low to maintain contact."

The tower told me to hold again. When they finally came back, the message was positive and very direct.

"Go outside and stand by your aircraft. Someone will be there momentarily."

All the Delta pilots followed me out to the Luscombe. Some said they had flown Luscombes at one time, and they were complimentary. A white Jeep with a large "Follow Me" sign on the back suddenly screeched to a stop behind my plane.

The man was wearing a head set and white coveralls. Pointing at me, he yelled, "Are you the pilot?" I nodded in the affirmative. "You follow me. We are going to get you out of here. Now! And under no circumstance will you use your transmitter."

He wheeled around and drove off down the tarmac. It was against regulations to start the engine by pulling your own prop (hand turning the propeller. My Luscombe didn't have a starter.) I was in enough trouble without adding more violations, so I waited.

The Jeep came back. The man seemed furious. "I told you to follow me."

I said, "Somebody's got to pull my prop."

He said, "What the hell are you talking about?"

One of the airline pilots said, "He doesn't have a starter. I'll do it." The pilot helped me turn the plane around facing the tarmac, and he pulled the prop. The engine started immediately. I tried to keep up with the Jeep, but he was going faster than I could go, and still keep the plane on the ground. When he finally stopped at the intersection to the south, east-west runway, I caught up. He jumped out of the Jeep and said, "Go!"

There was a Pan Am 707 flight about to touch down at the west end of the same runway. I held. I was not about to pull out and compete with that monster on the same runway, even though the strip was three-quarters of a mile long. When the Pan Am flight rolled out and would normally have turned off, onto the taxi-way, the man in the Jeep was forced to transmit to Pan Am 73. I had my receiver on and heard the conversation. He said, "Will Pan Am 73 pull on the right hand ramp and hold."

The pilot answered back. "Ground control, I hope you have a good reason. This thing is drinking fuel."

The controller said, "Pan Am, there is a tiny aircraft to your immediate port."

The pilot answered, "Got it in the sights. A cute little bird." Then in a tone of patronizing gallantry he said, "Pan Am is honored to relinquish the right of way to the little bird."

The man in the Jeep gave me a wave with his hand-held flag, with a flourish worthy of the starting flag at the Indianapolis Five Hundred. I put the throttle full forward and was airborne in less than the width of the runway.

When I lifted-off, high enough to clear the terminal and adjacent buildings, Ft. Lauderdale was saying, "One Eight Kilo, what is your position?"

I responded, "I am ten miles south-southwest of your field. They instructed me to fly directly to their field. They then cleared the area, giving me priority for a direct approach.

I landed and tied the Luscombe down, got my plane's airworthiness certificate and my pilot's license, and walked over to the tower. I climbed the stairs and confronted the two men who were obviously waiting for me. I said, "I don't know what you or the Civil Aviation Authority plans to do. And I don't really care. Here is my license and the plane is out there."

The older of the two waved my documents away, and said, "Sir, it has been a perfectly normal evening here. Miami has forgotten any unusual happenings tonight. We have forgotten anything that might have occurred, and I would suggest most sincerely that you forget whatever it is that you seem to be concerned about."

I went over to the terminal and met my friend. I was exhausted. My friend said he was beginning to worry, but then decided I was probably held up in traffic at Ft. Pierce, and had to take off later than I had planned. I asked him when he thought the Cuban missile crisis would be resolved. He said the military had everything pinned down in south Florida to the extent that nothing could move without them being on it in minutes.

There was one other occasion when it was necessary to land without knowing where I was.

It had a better ending than the Miami International incident.

In Leesburg, my wife, Pat, and I had four boys in school. We had sold the doublewide factory at the end of the first year to Chance Vought, and I was retained under the sales contract in an advisory capacity. I continued to process the documents with the Luscombe, and represented the company in promotions. The change necessitated flying three or four days a week. Pat would drop me off at the airport, and I would return when the day's business was finished. We lived on the edge of Lake Griffin, only a half-mile from the local airport.

Our German shepherd became so familiar with my plane that, even though there was constant local air traffic over the house, the dog recognized the sound of the Luscombe and knew I was coming long before I came into sight. I would fly over the lake and the dog would be racing from the back door to the car and back to the door, barking in a desperate effort to tell my wife to go to the airport and pick me up. (The dog was allowed to ride along with Pat.) It was a good time for my family and me. I flew, and painted in my spare time.

I had so many hours in *The Gnat* that I wore it like a suit of clothes. I knew what its limits were and stayed alert, always expecting the unexpected. In late summer, Florida's thunderstorm production was running at peak capacity. Every day I flew, there were active cells operating by midmorning, and increasing in size and quantity as the day progressed. I avoided the forward sides and their down drafts (We didn't call it wind-sheer then.). They were always there. It was normal to fly a zig-zag course from one point to another. Occasionally, I was forced to lay over in south or west Florida because of squall lines. Everyday, Lucille reminded me of the power of thunderstorms; as if it was the first time she had emphasized the subject.

Some days, the storms would play out in the afternoon or drift out over the Gulf, creating perfect night-flying conditions over the state. On other occasions, I skirted the active cells at night, and generally, I avoided night flights.

On a particular evening, I elected to attempt to fly home because of some activity that seemed important. There were electrical storms along the general flight path, but they seemed to be dying out. I took off about eight o'clock from a small field near Pompano, and found a corridor about twenty miles wide in the direction of Leesburg. For the first half hour, it was clear sailing. Then, it began to close in.

I picked my way for another half-hour, and was confronted with a line of thunderstorms blocking any hope of continuing in the direction of Leesburg. Oh well, I thought, I am not going home tonight. I will turn back and fly home early in the morning. I did a hundred-and-eighty-degree turn, and discovered the storms had closed in behind me. Boots' second rule of survival was, "When you have a problem, put your mule on the ground and then deal with it."

There were no towns or villages, not even a single light from an isolated ranch house. The only sign of human habitation was a two-lane highway running north and south, less than a mile to the east of my position. It appeared to be my first and only option to get on the ground. Lucille reminded me that the thunderstorms were converging in on us. I told her if she wanted to help, she could create me an airport. She said she didn't create.

I had three or four minutes to get on the ground before I would be caught in the violent winds and rain, and possibly golf-ball-sized hail that were common to the leading edge of the storms. When I banked towards the highway, I saw another road intersecting with the highway a half-mile to the north, marked only by scattered car lights. There was a filling station or small truck stop at the intersection. I thought, I don't know exactly what intersection that is, but me and *Gnat* are going to be their guest in a few short minutes.

I nosed down sharply, planning to land back from the intersection in order to avoid any power lines that might be across the road. Without landing lights, I picked a semi-trailer-truck because I thought he would be less likely to panic and pull off the road and leave me in the dark. The wind buffeted the Luscombe, but I was able to keep it in line with the road. I throttled *The Gnat* to a speed slightly faster than that of the truck and let down over the trailer and cab, clearing the hood by a small margin.

Huge drops of rain landed simultaneously with my touchdown on the highway. The truck stayed a short distance behind, while I power landed and taxied just below flying speed.

My next goal was to reach the intersection and the small truck stop before a car came meeting us. That was not to be. A car turned south at the crossroad, coming in our direction. It was probably the only vehicle to come off the side road and go south that night. I had no choice. The road was only two lanes wide. I hit the left brake and rudder hard, bringing the wings parallel to the road, with the tail wheel in the ditch in order to clear the southbound lane.

The truck slowed as if we had practiced the maneuver dozens of times. He left his bright lights on, partially blinding the oncoming driver. Thus, although the propeller extended a little over the center lane as the car whizzed by, I am sure there is a driver somewhere in the country that does not know he passed an airplane that night.

I swung back onto the highway with the truck "in tow," lighting my way. A small, four-unit motel, painted white with dark-green trim, was directly behind the truck stop. I taxied between some parked trucks, using the illumination from the lightning, around to the backside of the motel, putting the prop right up to the wall on the downwind side. The sky had opened and the deluge of water, whipped into stinging pellets by gusts of wind, came down in sheets. Me and the Luscombe were safely on the ground.

The next order of business was to find out where we were and to get a place for me to spend the night. I got out, locked the door and ran around to the front of the motel and into the little office. There was, of course, no reason to run because I was wet through and through in the few short steps to the motel door.

A massive woman sat in a wicker chair that looked as if it had sagged and bulged over the years in an effort to accommodate its occupant. The lone light bulb suspended from the ceiling provided enough light to illuminate a tennis court. I asked, "Do you have a room?"

She countered, "You got cash money?"

I said, "Yes, ma'am."

"That will be four dollar . . ." She was interrupted by a barefoot man, wearing only a pair of trousers, who ran in, soaking wet, and looking like he had been kissed by a ghost.

"Maud, they is a real aeroplane out here. It come right up to the window back of my room." He gestured back toward the door. "It is a real aeroplane, came in right out of this storm. And it is setten' right out there behind your wall."

The woman jumped up and said, "Let me see the thing." The two of them ran out into the rain. I stood there in the bright light, bewildered. I didn't believe a Luscombe could create such a commotion. The man and the motel keeper came back in, dripping water, and stomping their feet. She was saying, "Well, I'll be. I'll be. Well, I'll be."

The man looked at me as if he saw me for the first time. "You're the pilot!" It was not a question. It was more like a sworn statement. I nodded in the affirmative. The man pointed his finger at me, looked first at me, and then the lady. "He's the pilot." He looked back at me and then to her and repeated, "He is the pilot."

A second red-haired lady, wearing a bar apron, ran in the door. She looked at me and said, "Don't keep him over here. Everybody says bring him to the bar." Big Mama grabbed me by the hand and led me out into the rain, through puddles that ran in over my shoe tops.

As I was being pushed through the door, I asked, "What is the name of this place?"

Big Mama said, "Honey, you are the first person ever to land a airplane in Yeehaw Junction!"

The minute we were inside the door, somebody put a beer in my hand. I was shuffled around, slapped on the back, and had my hand shook repeatedly. I didn't have time to connect names with faces before having my hand seized by another customer.

Big Mama had transformed into the hostess, and she was determined to introduce me to the dozen or more men and women in the bar, although I didn't hear a single name. The jukebox that had been turned up to drown out the noise of the storm was still playing full blast. The patrons continued to slap me on the back and all talked at one time.

An older man pushed his way through the crowd and confronted me almost as if he was going to be hostile. He stood for a second, then put his hand out. "I would've been sorry the rest of my life if I hadn't got the chance to shake your hand "

I said, "Is that right?"

He hollered above the racket. "I been driving a big rig for near thirty years an' I ain't never had anything like that airplane of yours just appearing there in front of my windshield. Feller, you nigh got my bulldog (the radiator ornament on Mack trucks)." He laughed deep and snorted. "Hell, if he wuz real, you'd scared him to death." I tried to thank him for his truck lights, but he protested. "I wuz burning them anyway an you done give me some 'em to think on for the next hundred thousand miles."

The redheaded woman brought me a second glass of beer, and kissed me full on the mouth. I thought, Uh-oh, and looked around for some man that might get jealous, but no one seemed to care.

I know Charles Lindbergh was welcomed when he landed in Paris, but it couldn't have been more sincere or festive than the night I landed in Yeehaw Junction.

Big Mama put me to bed about three o'clock. She then got me an electric fan from her office, and said there wouldn't be any charge for the room.

Being a hero was more tiring than I thought. I intended to slip out just at daylight and be gone before the Florida Highway Patrol made me pay a fine for landing on U.S. Highway 441. In addition, I would have to remove the wings and tow the Luscombe forty-six miles to the nearest airport.

I woke at ten minutes of nine, jumped out of bed, put on my clothes and shoes, and dashed out to the plane. A young Florida Highway Patrolman was peeping in the window. I thought, here comes a citation and a towing bill to Lake Wales.

When I walked up he said, "Is this your plane?"

I said, "Yes."

He looked it over from one end to the other, then asked, "How much does it cost to fly one of the things?"

I said, "Practically nothing."

"I been thinking about getting one," he said, while he looked inside a second time.

It seemed as good a time to leave as I would get. I asked if he would mind holding the traffic on the highway. I explained I did not want to interfere with the flow of traffic.

He said, "Sure. I'll get someone here to hold the north bound, and I will run down the road and block the south bound." He started to his patrol car.

I said, "These are mighty nice people here in Yeehaw Junction."

He answered, without looking back, "The finest."

I took off feeling good about myself, airplanes and people. I have not had the opportunity to visit Yeehaw Junction since that night, but I have a lot of good friends there.

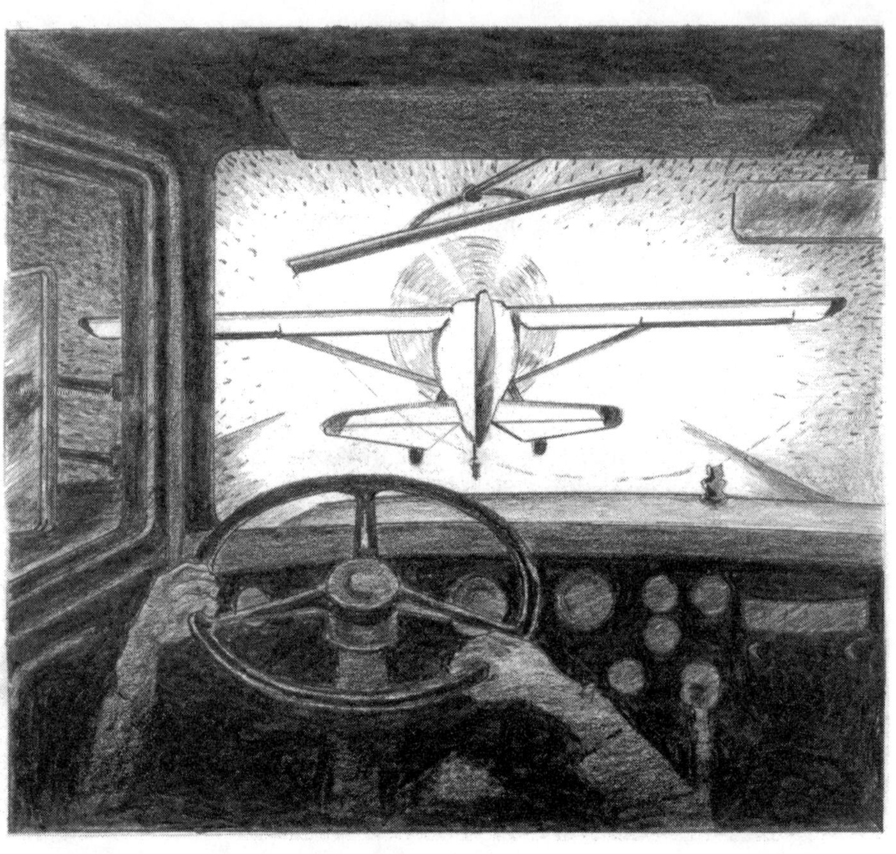

Chapter 13

THE GREAT MANSO EXPEDITION

When Pat and I lived in Miami, I was fascinated with the city's links to Central and South America. Floridians were vaguely aware of the business and tourism that were quietly developing between Miami and its southern neighbors. In the advertising agency where I worked, we did a poster for Pan American Airways, designed to attract Spanish-speaking tourists to the United States; the headline was simply U.S.A. The art consisted of exaggerated skyscrapers extending up from snow white beaches, and neon-lit shopping centers. The ad campaign was part of a new postwar America reaching out to foreign markets.

For me, it was the opening of new horizons. On weekends and holidays, my co-workers frequently took the twenty-nine-dollar, round-trip excursion flights to Cuba and the Bahamas. To me, the idea of traveling abroad was wild and exciting. Nearly twenty years passed before Lucille and I would have an opportunity to explore the Caribbean, Central and South America became a reality. Several ventures into Central America, coupled with my inherent desire to see what lies beyond every hill, eventually led me to Argentina, and ultimately to a glacier-fed stream that was both mysterious and unforgettable. No place on this planet is more dissimilar to Cross Creek than southern Argentina and the Andes Mountains. At least that was my impression during the eighteen years I visited there. However, deep into those mountains, the human equation revealed a commonality that was surprisingly similar.

My foray into Argentina began unexpectedly. In the early '70s, I was offered an opportunity to do marketing for a ski resort in Bariloche, a small town eight hundred miles southwest of Buenos Aires. I jumped at the chance. Lucille objected, pointing out that I knew nothing of the people or their government, and that I especially knew nothing about the magnitude of the longest and largest mountain range in the world. I told her, with an air of condescending patience, that I had climbed mountains in Hokkaido, and had driven on the Blue Ridge Parkway. And as to the people in the Andes, they could not be very different from Costa Ricans, Japanese, or Ainus. Thankfully, my wife, Pat, has a bit of the wanderer in her own Italian and Irish blood, so she agreed, on the condition that she could come down anytime. Lucille, always wanting to be sure that she was not being taken for granted, said she and Pat were like the caboose on a fast train; their only consolation lay in the hope that the next station would be warmer or cooler than the last one.

After eight thousand miles and a nine-and-a-half-hour flight from Miami, Pat and I landed in Buenos Aires, a modern city nearly the size of New York. The traffic was faster and wilder than New York. As a matter of fact, the traffic was faster and more reckless than it was in Rome or any place I have been. The streets and boulevards were wider, and the men and women were more fashionably dressed than the people back home. That was the good side. On the down side, the economy was coming apart with inflation that managed to stay over one hundred per cent annually. There were two years when I was there that it exceeded four hundred percent. The peso and the government got progressively worse as the country went from dictators to anarchy, and finally to a military government.

The amazing thing was the way that the people reacted to their government and the chaotic economy. They went on vacations, started new businesses, and partied more than we did in America. Confused, I asked a friend of mine, "How can your country tolerate such conditions?"

He laughed and answered my question with a question. "Do you know the problem with Americans?"

I said, "No."

He said, "You do not know how to ignore your government. Here, we pay no attention. They raise the taxes; we do not pay. They make regulations; we pay them no mind. If the traffic light is red, it is not a reason to stop, it is only a signal to look for the police."

I told him that sounded similar to my native Cross Creek.

He said he never heard of Cross Creek.

My interest was primarily in the country rather than Bariloche, a Swiss-like town with a population of 28,000, situated on the eastern slope of the southern Andes. Paved roads and the twentieth century ended there. To the south, there were little frontier towns, comparable to those we associate with America's old west, separated by fifty to one hundred miles of semi-arid landscape. To the west, mountains rise like a wall. Cerulean lakes, really inland seas, snuggle between magnificent snow-capped mountains. Bariloche is like Switzerland without the Swiss manicuring. Lush forests, similar to those along the northwest coast of the United States, slope up to the timberline. It is truly one of the most beautiful places I have ever seen.

Bariloche is off the beaten path for American tourists, so conversations in English were rare. However, all Argentines with high school speak some English, and generally welcome the opportunity to practice their English-American vocabulary. My Spanish is and has always been terrible. My friends say that it is compounded by my southern Cracker drawl.

When I asked about the mountains and wilderness areas south of the town, the men in the cocktail lounges said, "Señor, you do not want to go there. It is rough country, and many bad people there would do you great harm. The people there are gauchos. They carry big knives and they cut your throat in a minute. Señor, stay away from the gauchos." Everyone nodded in agreement.

Fantastic scenery and trout fishing were a greater temptation than the warnings of the townspeople. When I could steal the time, I fished and explored the lakes and streams, venturing further and further south. The country folks were mostly part-time gauchos who supplemented their families' existence with small herds of sheep and family gardens. In addition, they fished the river under questionable legal circumstances, and tended cattle owned by upper-class families who lived in the cities along the east coast.

The country people were shy and slow to become friendly with strangers, especially English-speaking strangers. The smallest smattering of English was rare, but they liked my pictures and sign language. These people were definitely not the type that would cut your throat. I have an inborn aversion to cold weather, so I made sure I did not go to Argentina until mid-September, which is late spring. I planned all my activities to be completed by mid-April, before the frigid Antarctic winds blew in from the south.

I probably would have moved on to another job, but I was fascinated with the area south of Bariloche. On each successive trip, I fished and explored further south into the area where the city dudes had said the people were bad. Each mile was more beautiful than the last, revealing magnificent mountains and small lakes and streams. From week to week throughout the short growing season, the foliage and the mountains themselves changed colors.

One particular stream fascinated me and although I did not know at it the time, it would eventually lead me to one of the most fascinating places I have ever known. Each visit, I started at the place I had left off before. The stream, the Manso, originated from a glacier on the sixteen-thousand-foot Mt. Tronador, and ran south forty kilometers, then abruptly turned west through the mountains toward the Pacific. A narrow road veered off in the direction the stream flowed, so I followed it up a perilous incline that in some places appeared impossible for my feeble vehicle to climb. I was driving a lowly Rastrohara, an Argentine-manufactured truck. Eventually, I came to the crest, and was treated to a spectacular view of a valley that extended several miles westward. I later learned that the stream I had followed, at the point it turned westward, was classified as a river.

The valley had a serene beauty, with the Manso meandering through the center. Small herds of sheep and a few cows grazed in open areas near the river. There were no fences. The only sign of human habitation was an isolated homestead consisting of a rough-lumber cottage, a corral, and a small garden, a mile down the valley. The place looked like a western movie set, depicting the old west in the mid-eighteen-hundreds. I followed a three-rut road that was obviously used by horses and ox carts, because the center rut was deeper than the ruts on either side. I passed a woman and a boy who were hanging clothes on a line. Busying themselves, without looking up, they pretended not to notice me.

On my third trip to the valley, I picked up a boy about ten or twelve, walking along the road. He did not speak any American, and I of course did not speak enough Spanish to communicate. I did my sign language bit, explaining that I was interested in fishing in the river. He looked from side to side like a passenger on a tourist bus, then picked up my sketchbook and thumbed through it nodding his head in approval. I am sure he enjoyed the ride because he let me pass the place he was obviously going. When he asked to stop, he got out, thanked me, and went trotting back in the direction we had come.

After I met the boy, the people I saw waved and appeared to be friendly. It caused me to remember when I was a kid growing up at Cross Creek. I would meet some of Marjorie Rawlings' friends, and rush around the area, giving my critique of the strangers to everyone. Apparently, I had passed the boy's approval rating.

On a Sunday in late summer, I went to the Manso valley, determined to explore as far as I could. I drove the Argentine truck. The weather was perfect. I packed a lunch, and wore light clothes, intending to return to Bariloche before night. I stopped from time to time and explored the areas where the river separated from the road. Half way down the valley, I passed a spot where the river widened to thirty yards and was deep. I caught two trout and released them.

Across the river, I saw a family consisting of a man, a woman, a teenage boy, a girl about ten, and two small children, walking along a path. They appeared to be wearing their Sunday clothes, and enthusiastically waved to me. I supposed they were on their way to visit friends or possibly to some kind of religious service. When they were fifty meters past me, the mother and father picked up the small children and put them up onto their shoulders. Then they waded into the cold, crystal-clear river that was more than a meter deep. Because of the current, they came out near where I was sitting, and then continued toward the homestead at the upper end of the valley. It was a warm day with low humidity. I surmised they expected the low humidity and sun to dry their clothes before they reached their destination.

The valley at the head of the Manso became an obsession to me. I looked forward to returning, and manipulated my work to spend as much time in the valley as possible. Even Lucille seemed happy. I understand Manso means "tranquil," and no name could be more appropriate. I decided I would explore as far as it was possible to go in my flimsy vehicle, and then walk the two or three miles to the end of the valley.

I set out in high spirits, trying to sing "The Bear Went Over the Mountain."

The open areas gave way to a dense forest, and the road became no more than a trail that had only been traversed by ox carts. I decided that I should turn around, park the truck, and continue on foot. I picked a spot to negotiate a u-turn. When I attempted to back the truck up, it made a loud clanking sound, and would not go in reverse. I thought, J.T., you have got yourself a problem.

Lucille did not appear to be anywhere in the vicinity. After a half hour of jiggling and working the shift, it was obvious that I would not be able to back the truck up, without a major repair. And that would have to be done more than sixty miles back through the mountains in Bariloche.

Without a reverse gear, there was no choice but to continue on, following the vague ruts, and hoping to find a place wide enough make a u-turn. The sun had moved behind the mountains, causing the forest to be dark, just like my mood. I was forced to keep going further and further.

Finally, in desperation, I found a place in which I believed I could maneuver the vehicle between the trees, to turn it back in the direction I had come. I got out and picked up the limbs and debris that would be in the truck's path. Convinced that I could do it, I climbed back into the truck, started the engine, and began moving forward in low gear as cautiously as possible, over the roots and mud bogs.

The Rastrohara had a turning radius like a battleship. Two-thirds of the way through the turn, it became clear that the turning radius was not short enough. The truck was on a path leading directly into a large tree. There was no jack to lift the front, which would enable me to tip it to the side. I rolled some logs at an angle, to veer the front to the left. It didn't work. The front of the truck moved closer to the tree. My situation was hopeless. I could not turn the truck around. The vehicle was pointed at a tree and could not back up.

I sat there frustrated, with no options but to walk back the twenty-five or more miles to the main road. Even when I got there, the chance of a car coming along was slim. All things considered, I had no choice. I gathered uneaten bits of my lunch, and tried to think of anything that would help me on the long walk. I sat for a few more minutes, feeling sorry for myself. I had known the truck was a piece of junk. I had only myself to blame. I wished Lucille were around.

At the moment I started to get out of the truck and begin walking, I heard a snorting sound. I glanced at some movement in the rear view mirror. Five gauchos were coming up behind the truck. To use an expression of my friend, Rip Torn, they looked like they came directly from central casting. They were on horseback, and the leader rode in the front, with his companions following, two by two. They were wearing the classic gaucho flat-brim hats with chin straps and chaps. I was sure each one had the traditional 12-inch knife tucked under his belt in the center of his back.

"Lucille, where are youuu?"

Looking like the queen's honor guard the horses stood proud with their chins tucked in,. They stopped a few feet from the truck. I thought, these could be the mean people that would "keel" me. Nevertheless, I was glad to see them. In my situation, I was glad to see anyone.

I jumped out and started rattling off about my problem in Cracker American. They just sat staring at me like granite statues in a park. It seemed impossible that five horses and five riders could be so still. Not one of the horses switched his tail or wiggled an ear.

Then I realized they were not looking at me, but at the truck pointed at the center of the tree. The ridiculousness of my situation was obvious, and I was desperate. I did not want to walk twenty-five miles in the dark and maybe another forty the next day.

The gauchos had two options—they could kill me or help me get the truck turned around. I, of course, opted for turning the truck. In my best sign language, I tried to demonstrate the gearshift and that it was broken and would not go in reverse. And in the event that one of them might understand a smattering of English, I explained each movement of my sign language verbally. I threw in some of the Spanish words I knew, along with a few words in Japanese, reincarnated from my military sojourn.

There was no response. They just sat there.

I repeated my performance of the broken gearshift, the need to turn the truck around, and that the time was late and I needed to be back in Bariloche. Still no reaction. Nothing. I had never heard such silence. In a desperate effort to see if they were hostile or if it was a simple communication problem, I went to the front of the truck and attempted to push it backward.

The leader raised his hand and snapped his finger with a sweeping motion. The last rider on the left rear broke ranks and moved toward the back of the truck. He took his lariat, made of plaited leather, and threw it around the rear bumper. He then started backing his horse.

I tried to tell the leader that the little horse could not move the big truck in such soft ground. He ignored me. The horse had his rump almost on the ground, pushing with all four legs, and slowly pulled the truck around. I jumped on the running board and steered it into a position facing the road. The gaucho flipped his lariat off the bumper and returned to his position in the group.

I have never been so grateful and indebted and frustrated in my life. I tried to thank the stone faces, but realized the futility of anything I might do. When I no longer needed her, Lucille appeared and suggested a gift. There were four packs of cigarettes in the glove compartment. I grabbed them and handed them to the leader. Without looking back or changing his regal bearing, he took them and pitched them, one pack at a time, back over his shoulder. One of the gauchos caught them, single-handed, and gave a pack to the other three members of the rear guard. All five horses walked away into the forest, as if they were a single unit. As inexplicably as they had appeared, they were gone.

I could not believe they had been there. It was as if the whole event had been staged and rehearsed. There was the distinct possibility Lucille had created the entire episode. After they left, she had most certainly made herself scarce.

Driving back, it dawned on me that the gauchos had acted like the Cross Creek fishermen in Florida when they were pulling a joke on a stranger. The more I thought about it, I was sure that I had been the object of gaucho humor. At that very moment, they were probably all splitting their sides, laughing at the silly gringo who drove his truck up to a big tree, and then did a vaudevillian pantomime performance, speaking in an unknown tongue, for some cowboys on their way home from work.

The truck episode did not stop me from going to the little valley on the upper Manso. During the next two summers, I became acquainted with the household of the mother and father of the boy I had met when I first discovered the area. The boy's name was Carlos Carro. His father, Alfredo Carro, was a gaucho and tended cows which were owned by a man who lived in Buenos Aires. The cattle roamed the mountains. In addition, Alfredo had a small herd of thirty sheep and twelve chickens.

He was a tall, slender man, about thirty-five, and had the look of a person who had lived his life outdoors. I was surprised to find he knew a few words of English from the five years he served in the military. He was patient with my pitiful Spanish. Our conversations sounded like two four-year-olds discussing the geographic idiosyncrasies of Mars.

Alfredo told me there were three families that lived within ten kilometers of his home, and then no others for more than twenty-five kilometers, in the interior of the mountains. Alfredo had never been to the place where the mountain people lived.

I never attempted to drive into the forest again, always choosing to park the truck where the road ended, and did my exploring on foot. There was an occasional encounter with someone on horseback or walking. They all spoke and looked at me with a subdued grin that clearly said, "You're the gringo who got his truck stranded in front of a tree."

At the end of the valley, a small creek, called the Rio Foyel, flowed into the Manso. It was a magical spot with a primitive swinging bridge that crossed the gorge to the opposite bank. I went there several times, intending to do a watercolor, but always elected to sit and savor the ethereal beauty of the time and the place: snow-capped mountains, waterfalls, and the sound of the creek merging with the river which eventually led to Chile and the Pacific.

I tried to find a vantage point by climbing up to a ledge where the Manso was bordered by vertical walls of rock. With a lot of effort, I managed to slither onto an outcropping, and was rewarded with a spectacular view. Water and ice had carved smooth abstract crevices into the granite walls, reflecting millions of years of seasonal floods and drought. The Manso had narrowed and become restless, anxious to be on its way. A hundred meters into the gorge, a mist rose in a shaft of sunlight, creating a spectrum of colors like a curtain marking the end of visibility from the valley. I could hear the roar of the river, further downstream, as it began plummeting the two thousand feet before it finally mixed with the tides of the Pacific.

I had the feeling of one who has missed the last act in a good play. I told Lucille, "I have some unfinished business here. I don't know how, but I am coming back to follow that river through to the Pacific. It is like the Venus DeMilo wrapped in a beach towel. I want to see it all."

She said, "Don't be overly dramatic."

I returned to the States shortly after I had found the end of the Manso valley. My work in Argentina had ended. Normally, Bariloche and the Manso River would have become a faded memory, but I was obsessed with the portion that I had not seen.

Alfredo had told me that there were three or four families living down the river, in the very heart of the mountains. I had asked him if it was possible to follow the river to the ocean. He said, "I believed it is possible, but there would be many problems. He didn't know anyone personally who had. "We hear rumors of political refugees coming through, but no one sees them." I told him I would return and we would go through as soon as I could arrange it. He gave me a cynical look and said, "Sure, amigo."

Immediately after my return to the States, I flew to Nova Scotia to consult with a monastery on the construction of a retreat they planned to build in the mountains of Colorado. They lived in the monastery, Nova Nada, in almost complete silence. One of the monks was allowed to discuss construction of the proposed project with me for two hours each morning. The rest of the day was supposed to be spent in silence, contemplating the wonders of nature, the Creator, and specifically the meaning of the term, "to be."

The days were long and there was two feet of snow on the ground, so I paced the floor of my little one-room cabin. Lucille loved it and suggested we stay for a year. While I was there, I met a young lady who was on retreat. Apparently, she also had a problem with the silence and after two days, we cheated and talked. She was a photographer for a travel magazine. Naturally, I told her about the Manso and my obsession to return and explore the river. She was fascinated and said I should.

The day I was returning home, she said, "I can get you an appointment with the editor of *National Geographic*. You should go to Chicago and check their library, and if your river has not been explored, the editor will be interested."

Before I left the monastery, the monks had a special talk night, with a going-away dinner followed by a festive party. I thanked them for their hospitality and read them a poem I had written while contemplating the words "to be." It ended with these lines:

"I know nothing of meditating quietly,
Or of things 'to be.'
There is, alas, one thing I've learned,
Silence is not for me."

Two weeks later, I was in Chicago at the National Geographic offices. A thorough search of their library revealed only one reference to the Manso River, and that was an article in the early part of the century. The story was about the exploration of minerals in Argentina. The writer referred to a rumor of diamonds being found in a place called the Manso River area. The rumor was found to be false, ending his investigation without going there. I got an appointment with Bill Graves, the editor. He appeared surprised they didn't have more data on the river. He offered to pay my expenses to go back to survey the Manso, photograph it, and report back on the area and its people.

Before leaving Washington, I called at the Argentine and Chilean embassies. Relations between the two countries were not good at the time, and I wanted to be able to cross the border without problems. The Chilean embassy gave me a letter of introduction to the Governor, a general, of the Reloncavi Province, which was where the Manso flowed into the estuary, joining the Pacific. The Argentine embassy gave me a letter to the Director of Tourism in the Provence of San Carlos De Bariloche, asking him for his cooperation in my venture.

A week later, I was on my way to the Manso with a backpack, and more film than I had shot collectively in my life. I arrived in Santiago and caught a train to Puerto Montt, the closest town to the mouth of the Manso. The Santiago Opera was going on tour and were the only passengers in the ancient car. Lucille loved it. The opera singers sang and drank most of the night, making toasts to me, my wife, my children, the United States, Florida, and even Cross Creek. The tenor, who was a good second for Pavarotti in voice and physique, had read *The Yearling* and *Cross Creek*. The following morning, understandably, everyone slept until noon.

In mid-afternoon, we passed Mt. Orsorno, the most beautiful mountain I have ever seen. An hour later, we were in sight of our destination, Puerto Montt, a town perched on crescent cliffs, which faced the Gulf of Aeneid. The train slowed and crept carefully down the steep grade leading to the town.

Lucille alerted me to the screeching and tearing sound of steel rails and wheels. It was a sound we had heard in Costa Rica, when a train we were riding there had jumped the tracks. Although we were only moving twenty or thirty miles an hour, I knew the windows did not have safety glass.

I grabbed the tenor's full-bodied wife, a soprano, and dove into the aisle. Her husband was preparing to attack me when the car rolled over onto its side. He, of course, came tumbling down on top of us, placing me in the middle of a soprano-tenor sandwich. With a lot of grunting and dust, the car stopped.

No one was hurt, and I could always say I was, for a brief moment, intimately associated with a world-renowned opera company. We climbed out a window and walked the last mile to Puerto Montt, with the entire opera company singing the march from *Aida*. It seemed a most proper way to begin the great Manso expedition.

I presented my letter of introduction to the Governor. He was polite and offered me anything I needed to complete my mission. I asked for a plane and a pilot to reconnoiter the Chilean side of the Manso. The next morning, provided with a Grumman propjet and an army pilot, we worked out a flight plan to survey and photograph the lower Rio Manso, known as the Rio Puelo in Chile.

Half an hour later, I was strapped into a harness that allowed me to hang partially out of the rear door. My first look at the lower Manso was breathtaking, to say the least. The pilot was bold and brave. I photographed the river at levels that would have been the envy of Boots, my old American crop-dusting instructor. At speeds in excess of a hundred-forty miles-an- hour, we made five passes.

There was a small village near the mouth of the river, but no sign of houses. Further inland, in the area of the Argentine border, I counted three houses perched on knolls between the mountains. A chain of waterfalls, like a descending staircase, cascaded down the river to the sea. At one point, my glasses were sucked out of my pocket and lost in the rocks and forest below.

It was a great flight. Lucille expressed her sympathy for the Chilean pilot's guardian angel.

The following morning, I crossed over to Argentina at a point less than fifty miles north of the Manso. The trip was the most beautiful one-day trip I have ever taken. I was witness to emerald glaciers, crystal lakes, and majestic mountains.

In Bariloche, I rented a car, bought some snacks, and set out to the Manso Valley. My friend, Alfredo Carro, welcomed me like a long-lost brother. I asked if I could hire him and his horses to guide me across the mountains to the mouth of the Manso in Chile. He said it was a trip he too had always wanted to make. However, he thought he should discuss it with his wife before making a decision. They had a private conference, then she poured three glasses of wine.

He gave me a glass and said, "We are friends and it is not necessary to pay. But I think you might give me your American Stetson hat if all goes well on the trip."

I agreed to meet him at four a.m. the following morning. At that latitude in midsummer, it is daylight at four and twilight until ten.

When I arrived, Alfredo was waiting at the corral with the horses saddled. He smiled and said, "I told the señora you would be early." I gave him my personal supplies, which included an extra shirt, a sweater, thirty rolls of film, and a copy of a *National Geographic* magazine that had an article with the western paintings of Charles Russell. He slipped them beneath a waterproof cover, which was on a neatly packed third horse.

Then, after saying goodbye to his family, he called his dog. I mounted with more effort than I would have preferred anyone to notice. After years of dreaming and weeks of waiting, we were on our way.

My horse was as anxious as I to get underway. She snorted lightly and moved off, following the packhorse, with Alfredo's horse leading the way. The gaucho saddle, consisting of several layers of sheepskins, was surprisingly comfortable.

I let the reins hang slack and whispered to the horse, "Old girl, you know more about these mountains than I do, so consider yourself on autopilot for the rest of the trip."

We rode through the forest at the lower end of the valley and passed the tree that had blocked my efforts to turn the truck around. Alfredo nodded in its direction, and gave me a knowing grin. Apparently, the tree had become a symbolic landmark of American stupidity.

At the place where the Manso entered the narrow gorge, we forded the river. I tucked my knees under my chin to avoid the cold water. On the far side, the horses entered a narrow trail and began climbing. Alfredo let his horse find his footing on the damp slippery rocks that led through heavy foliage, completely obliterating the overgrown path. For more than a half hour, I could not see the packhorse, or Alfredo, because of the growth. When we broke out into a clearing, Alfredo and the packhorse were waiting.

He said, "Your horse is the cautious one. She takes her time."

I patted her on the neck and told her, "It's O.K., girl. You're my kind of a horse."

We paralleled the river, following a seldom-used path down stream. The path continued to climb through dense hardwood forest that eclipsed the sun rising behind us. Occasionally, we caught a glimpse of the river, eight hundred feet, or more, below.

Five miles downstream, a one-room log cabin housed a soldier who was tending a small garden. The twelve-foot-by-twenty-foot plot was the first level ground I had seen since we left the valley. I showed him my passport. He didn't open it. He said his only concern was people that might come from Chile, going east.

He was the only person I saw in the area that was not clean and neat. I supposed if I were a soldier stationed for months in an outpost isolated from civilization, and expected to grow most of my own food, I would not care about appearances. There seemed to be a vague similarity between the lonely soldier and cosmonauts living in a space station. He said if he happened to be asleep when we returned, he would appreciate it if we did not wake him. We moved off, and he returned to his gardening.

When the sun was directly overhead, we stopped for lunch. Alfredo unpacked the ingredients for a delicious salad and homemade bread, all from the hidden recesses of his saddle, to go with the three liters of red wine attached to the packhorse. A man of subtle good taste, he selected a site for lunch by the river, beneath a primitive swinging bridge. He said he had never been to this place before.

The Manso in this area, for a few short yards, is tranquil. It abounds with rainbow and brown trout, wild ducks, and geese that show little, or no, fear of man. Alfredo showed me the track of a large wild cat. He said the cat was called *coldcola* in Spanish.

A patch of grass, the size of a small golf green, lay only a few feet above the rock floor and the swift current of the river. There was something serene about the place. The roar of falls was barely audible from upstream, the direction from which we had come. I sat in the warm sun while my gaucho friend gathered sticks to fire an *acedo* or barbeque.

He pulled a side of lamb from under the cover on the packhorse, and secured it on a stick over the fire. I was surprised at the fresh meat and asked where he had gotten it. He explained that it was his turn to furnish the *acedo* for the school's lunch, back in the valley. He had slaughtered the lamb before I arrived, and his son had taken the other half to school, along with a loaf of bread his wife had baked for the entire school's lunch.

I asked if the teacher prepared the *acedo*. He said no, the children do it. Although it sounded like a dumb question, I asked, "Do they have an *acedo* every day?"

He answered in a matter-of-fact tone, "Some days they prepare it with beef, but mostly it is lamb."

When the meat was a golden brown and smelled heavenly, Alfredo reached under his saddle and came out with two stemmed wine glasses. He poured the wine and raised his glass in a toast-like gesture.

I was dumbfounded. "You carry wine glasses under your saddle?"

He laughed. "No. This is a special occasion. It is tradition. We are both crossing these mountains for the first time."

We raised our glasses to the snow-capped peaks around us, as if they were our guests.

While we ate, I noticed a crude sign attached to a tree leaning over the river. Even if I could have read the Spanish words carved into it, time and weather had deteriorated it enough to make them illegible. Alfredo said he had heard of this place, and understood the bridge was a local source of great pride, having been constructed by voluntary local labor in memory of a woman who came to the area before the turn of the century. She was a folk hero.

He studied it and added, "Perhaps it is this place."

We skipped the usual siesta and continued, following the river. By three o'clock, the sun was lost behind the mountains. There were periods of time, up to an hour, in which we could not talk from horse to horse because of the roar of the river. The trail was narrow, and loose stones made the footing perilous. With their eyes wide and ears back, the horses cautiously crept forward. From time to time, Alfredo dismounted and led them past places where the path was littered with loose gravel. I was glad that Lucille was somewhere in the immediate vicinity.

About six-thirty, we reached an opening with small fields, each less than an acre, balanced on knolls between the almost vertical walls of the mountains. I asked Alfredo, "Why do they live on top of these knolls between the mountains?"

He said, "It is because the mountains are so high on the east and west sides of the gorge, that the sun does not shine long enough down in the bottom where the river flows, to farm. Up on the knolls, the sunlight is, maybe, three hours longer each day."

Two men and a boy were cutting wheat with hand sickles, binding them in bunches, and loading them on a cart pulled by an ox. They looked up for a moment and returned to their work as if we did not exist. Alfredo said, before I could ask, "The further you get into the mountains, the more the people are shy of strangers."

A quarter-mile farther, we came in sight of a wood-frame house roofed with hand-wrought shingles. It sat on wooden piers and was sided with clapboards split from logs. A porch stretched across the front, with a bench and two homemade chairs. Although the house was weathered by scores of harsh winters, without preservative coating, its builder's German ancestry was apparent. This later proved to be the home of the Santa Turra family.

I asked Alfredo if he would go to the house, tell the lady I was from the United States, and ask her if I could visit her home. He rode his horse to the yard gate and went up to the porch, surrounded by a flock of geese and three or more yard dogs. I took pictures and waited.

When he returned, he relayed what the lady said, that I would be welcome, but she would like it if I would give her a half hour to prepare for my visit. Alfredo said with an air of experience, "Women are like that. If she just finished cleaning, she would like to clean more before company comes." I supposed they would do the same thing if we were in China.

Señora Turra came to the steps to greet us. With the dogs mingling around our feet, and with a lot of difficulty, she introduced me to her German ancestry grandmother, daughter, twelve-year-old Sandra, and daughter, Anamaria Los

Angeles, age four. The lady shooed the dogs away, while explaining that one of the men in the field was her husband, the boy was her son, and the other man was a neighbor.

We were led into the combination dining and kitchen area, and given seats on comfortable homemade chairs. The house had never been painted, inside or out. However, the floors were fresh-mopped, and there was no sign of dust in any corner. I looked around and could not see anything that could not have come from the eighteenth century, with the exception of a cast iron wood stove. Mrs. Turra saw my interest and said the stove was purchased in Bariloche, brought in disassembled from the Manso valley by five men who carried it on their backs. It was a wedding present for her husband's grandmother, about a hundred years ago.

The older daughter, Sandra, served fresh bread, warm from the oven, and three kinds of delightful wild berry jellies, along with soft fresh churned butter. Then she asked if I drank tea. I said I did and the mother poured it in blue-and-white willow pattern cups. There was an air of sophistication about our little party. I was hungry and ate more than was polite. The seven-year-old claimed credit for picking the berries.

I thought of the long trek back to the Manso valley, and the sixty miles that separated the valley from a store. I asked Mrs. Turra, "How often do you go to the store?"

She said with a tone of polite dignity, "Every year. We go between the snow-melt and Christmas." With a slight shrug of her shoulders, she added, "Of course, I do not go every year, but the men do."

I asked, "What do they buy?"

Without hesitating, she said, "Cloth, thread, medicine, sugar, salt, and tea. Some years, the men get a little Christmas gift for the children." I sipped my tea with an added sense of appreciation, and a degree of shame. I was drinking next year's tea. When we had finished, Mrs. Turra showed me her home. The rooms were small and dark. There were two small fireplaces. I could not imagine how they endured the eight months of freezing Antarctic winds and snow.

Alfredo rode back and joined the men in the field until darkness was imminent, then he returned to the house. I watched as they fed and tethered the ox and cows. The dog herded a small flock of sheep and geese into a log crib. The men washed their hands and faces at an open well, then came into the house, after stomping the dirt from their shoes. Señor Santa Turra insisted I stay in their home. He said, grinning towards Alfredo, "Only a gaucho can sleep on the ground with a single blanket." I accepted.

I slept in a goose down bed until the sun came over the mountains. It was ten o'clock. The men were already working in the field. Alfredo was sitting on the steps with the horses saddled, waiting. He handed me a rein. "Riding horseback makes you sleep well, yes?"

I answered, "Yes."

The Turra family assured us we would be welcome to stop on our return. We continued down the knoll some two hundred yards to the small home of Señor Obdulio Gallardo. It was perched on the edge of the knoll. Alfredo said he had talked to the Turra men while I slept, and they had said I could learn all I wanted to know of the people who lived in the middle of the Andes from Señor Gallardo. The old man proved to be an variable encyclopedia of the history and culture of this spot, which had the isolation of a crater on another planet.

We rode past the Gallardo house, to the extreme end of the knoll. Alfredo pointed. "See there. The narrow point in the mountains, that is in Chile for sure. In this area, no one knows where we are. Argentina says we are in Argentina, and Chile says we are in Chile."

I asked, "Where do the people who live here say it is?" He said, "It is of no importance."

A thousand feet down, the Rio Manso sounded like storm surf along the Atlantic coast. If I had not flown over the lower portion of the river, I would not have believed the river could be so violent.

Gallardo told us it was only ten miles to the next home. Laughing, he said, "It is more like nine miles down and one mile up, then about 15 miles to the bay."

We left the horses at Obdulio's and continued on foot. Long before nightfall, we camped. I slept on the ground, rolled up in one of Alfredo's blankets.

It was treacherous descending the rocks and cliffs. We passed a house, but it was vacant. Then we came to Lake Tagus. I checked the maps and knew we were twelve kilometers from the Estarte Reloncavi, which connected to the Pacific. We had reached the mouth of the Manso, or the Pueblo as it is called on the Chilean side. Achieving the goal was only as great as the experience of getting there.

Even though the trail back was steep, we made good time, and slept in a shallow cave out of the wind and roar of the river. We spent another night on the trail because I was too tired to continue. I dreamed of sleeping the next night in the goose down bed at Señora Turra's.

When we arrived at Señor Gallardo's house, we had time to visit. He told us he was born here. His house was also built prior to the turn of the century. It was simple and practical. His father died in 1945, his mother in 1976, at 98 or 99 years of age. I asked Señor Gallardo why he never married.

"No woman," was his reply.

"Did you ever think of living some other place?"

"No. When I was young, it was necessary that I was here for my mother and father to survive. From what I hear, I wouldn't like it there." He pointed in the direction we had come.

I asked, "Have you been to the border?" He didn't understand. "To the place where Argentina and Chile meet?"

"No."

Like a fool, I asked, "Why?"

He answered, "No reason."

Alfredo laughed. "It's not important here." I understood why the proud man was reluctant to pursue an imaginary line stretching thousands of miles down the center of the longest mountain range in the world.

"We live in the Andes," he said, proudly.

"What do you want from the world outside?" I asked.

He pronounced his full name, "Obdulio Gallardo wants his picture." I gave him a Polaroid. He accepted it with a sense of reverence. "I will leave it so people will remember me when I join my ancestors."

After a moment, he continued, "Before you leave, I would like you to accompany me to a special occasion."

Alfredo and I followed him down a narrow trail, and then up to another small knoll. I was surprised there were ten men and women, and several children, gathered around a paling fence that had been freshly painted a light blue. A lone tree shaded the twenty-by-twenty-foot plot. Gallardo spoke to them in Spanish. They all nodded in my direction.

He then turned to me. "Everyone in this area comes here on this day each year to honor our families and especially the lady in the grave there."

Pointing to the center of the plot, where wild flowers were strewn over the mound, he said, "She is very special. She came here in nineteen-one. She was a German lady. She came to the region on foot with her three-year-old daughter. Her mission was to teach the five families that lived isolated in the heart of the mountains, to read the *Bible*. She lived with us for two years, working with the different families during the days and teaching them to read at night. She taught both day and night during the winters, when the snow was too deep to work. The little English I know, I learned from my mother, who learned from her. When she felt her mission had been finished, she planned to move to other isolated areas in the mountains and continue her teaching."

Gallardo continued, saying, "The families were grateful for the German lady, and for her going-away party, they had a picnic in her honor, at the swinging bridge where Alfredo tells me you had your acedo." His narration of the events was like a ballad that he had sung many times.

"Señor, the party was a happy time. They had an *acedo* of roast lamb and goat, served with their best wine. After eating, they sang, and read from the *Bible*, while the children played near the river. A splash, followed by screaming children, interrupted the festivities. The five-year-old daughter of the teacher had fallen into the river. Because of the swift current and continuous falls, everyone stood helplessly for a moment. Then, the horrified mother jumped into the swift current in a vain attempt to rescue her drowning daughter. They were both immediately swept down and over the great falls."

Señor Gallardo's narration made it seem as if the tragedy had happened only a day or two before that moment. He paused in an attempt to control his emotions. "Their bodies were recovered downstream, near the homes of the people she had taught. The people of the high mountains consider this spot a memorial to the German lady." He pointed to a crude weathered hand-carved sign attached to an ornately carved post, which stood at the head of the grave.

I asked what it said. "It is a tribute to the lady."

He did not read the name. "1905" was legible even to me, followed by a larger inscription which Alfredo interpreted, "She came only to give."

I asked, "Where is the little girl buried?"

Gallardo answered, "We buried her in her mother's arms. They are there together."

The group said a prayer, genuflected and then walked away in silence.

I asked Alfredo if he thought we could ride back to his home in the dark. He didn't ask why, but nodded yes. We said goodbye to Señor Gallardo and the Turra family.

I thought it was the appropriate time, so I handed my Stetson to Alfredo and said, "I think this is yours."

He put it on using both hands, adjusting it to a position of masculine dignity. He then tipped it in my direction and said, "Gracias, Señor. I will wear it with pride." We rode out two hours before dark. The hat looked more appropriate on him than it had on me.

There is zero air pollution in the southern Andes. It appeared that we were riding among the stars. As we looked down, the only light came from the horses' shoes, striking sparks on the rocks. The billions of stars seemed so low that one could reach out and touch them.

I tried to sum up my excursion into the heart of the Andes. I thought about the people I grew up with, and about Cross Creek. It was not so dissimilar. Like most places on earth, there is beauty in the grandeur of the scenery, and beauty in the joys, and even beauty in the tragedies that occasionally descend upon us. But it is the human spirit in its complexity and simplicity that is the awesome part of the universe.

Chapter 14

THE POPE, CRACKERS AND GERMAN ARISTOCRACY

If God didn't have a better sense of humor than any of us, he would have eliminated the human race at any time after Adam and Eve. I, of course, have no idea of the religion of the aboriginal inhabitancy of Cross Creek, nor if their God remotely resembled the more popular current versions. I do know that God and the Creek are closely related. The fishermen there looked upward when they failed to catch fish. Occasionally one fell overboard and uttered expressions that were not exactly flattering to any divine being. Generally, there have been as many versions of God as there have been residents at the Creek.

In the late 1800s, Cross Creek's first post-Indian settlers built a formidable church about one hundred yards east of the Creek. It had a ten-foot ceiling, novelty pine interior, a steeple, and an altar in the front. They equipped it with pews made of long leaf pine, and a modest amount of ornamentation. Just prior to the grand opening, the big freeze of the 1890's wiped out all the citrus, and so all the inhabitancy moved away, leaving only God and a few Crackers who struggled in to fill the deserted houses. The Cross Creek Methodist Church stood deserted for thirty or more years and was finally occupied by a deserving family that removed the pews and made it a home.

On one occasion, a missionary couple came and had services in a seven-by-fifteen-foot travel trailer. The local young'uns went every weeknight for a month, where they were taught *Bible* verses and served Kool Aid. I don't know whether the missionaries felt their good work was accomplished, or if they were called to Tampa or China. Their contributions to religion at the Creek were sincere and they deserved credit for their efforts.

My family and the Brices regularly attended church in Island Grove. The Methodists and the Baptists could only afford a minister every other Sunday. The Baptists had to attend the Methodist church on the Sundays when they were having preaching and the Methodists attended the Baptist on the alternate Sundays. The ecumenical coalition was necessary to have a large enough crowd to sing and take up the collection.

I liked the singing, but day dreamed through the sermons. It was a part of life.

The Grand Ol' Opry was on Saturday night, and there was morning and evening church on Sunday. The only exception was fifth Sundays (my favorite), when they didn't have church at either place. I was free to go visiting, fish, or do anything except play cards. Momma was not sure whether it was all right to go swimming on Sunday, but she gave in on that point. In the hot summer months, we went to Garrison Hammock over on Lochloosa Lake, and occasionally to Orange Springs. All in all, Sundays were O.K. The extraordinary Sunday dinner, and the freedom to play all afternoon, offset the elongated sermon on Sunday morning.

The Methodists felt they had a little more class, since their songbooks were thicker, and their pews were contoured (made to fit only one size). The Methodists only sprinkled their converts, but the Baptists ducked theirs all the way under in a pond. Dad called them "deep water Baptists." Some said they had pools inside the big Baptist churches in cities, but most of us didn't believe it.

There was no denomination at the Shriner's Hospital. We had Sunday school and ice cream on Sunday. So I assumed that all churches were like Baptist and Methodist, if there was any other kind.

In the third grade, I spent the weekend with my friend in Hawthorne. On Sunday morning, they put on their best clothes, and off we went to church. I assumed it would be the same as church in Island Grove.

I will never forget the sheer shock of going into that little church. They had colored glass on the windows, so it was impossible to see outside. There was a board-like low bench on the back of the pews near the floor. They had electricity and even though it was daylight, there were candles burning all across the front. The preacher came out wearing a costume that no man, and especially a preacher, would be caught wearing in public. It had tassels and lace around the sleeves, and gold embroidered designs all over it. There was smoke coming out of a pot, and somebody kept ringing a little bell. The congregation stood up, sat down, and kneeled on the little bench. Then to top it all, they spoke in an unknown tongue (Latin).

I was dumbfounded by it all and to be truthful, frightened. When we got outside, I asked my buddy what kind of church it was. He said it was Roman Catholic. There was one thing for certain: I was not going to tell my folks where I had been. I knew that if they found out I had been to such a place, they would never let me visit my friend again. That was my introduction to Catholicism.

Ten years later, my mother said something about Catholics and I played dumb. She said, "You ought to know. You used to go to mass the weekends you spent with your friends in Hawthorne." I couldn't believe she had known all the time.

Officially, I became a Baptist when I was going into the Army. I needed all the support I could get. In service, I went to church because it was civilian and reminded me of home, and maybe because there were girls there. Generally,

Lucille was in charge of my spirituality.

All that abruptly changed when I met Miss Patricia Apone. I would have married her if she had been Hindu, Muslim, and Catholic. She was Catholic. She went to mass on Sunday, and on all holy days. Catholics seemed to have a lot of collections and holy days. I went to a Protestant service on rare occasions when fish weren't biting, just to show her I had religion, too. Later, our kids went to Catholic schools when it was possible, but there was no conflict in our family. My momma attended all the baptisms and ceremonies, and said I was lucky to have a wife who had any religion.

The first real shocker came when our oldest boy, Nick, who was in his first year of college, called and said he had something important he had to discuss with me. My first thought was that the young fool was planning to get married in his first year of college. I had always told our kids that there were two things I expected from them, with no exceptions. They had to be honorable, and productive. Being honorable was not enough; they had to be productive, too. It was not an original philosophy; I borrowed it from my Dad.

Nick got on the phone and said, "Hello, Dad. I want your blessing on something that is important."

I was ready to say, "Wait four years and get a job!"

He said, "I have decided I want to become a priest."

I sat there holding the phone. I could not implore the honorable statute and I couldn't use the non-productive clause on him. I asked if the commitment was irrevocable. He said he would go to seminary for eight years, and then the commitment would be final. I was stunned, but kind of proud. I said, "O.K. It's your life."

Before my son was ordained a priest, I joined the Catholic Church. While Pat and Momma and Lucille all approved, all my kids cried foul. They said they had to study catechisms and go through all manner of ceremonies, while all ol' Dad had to do was just go over to his buddy, the monsignor, and shoot the breeze for a while.

My Masonic friends said the Catholics wouldn't let me in. My Catholic friends said the Masons and Shriners would not let me be a Catholic. I checked with the hierarchy of both, and they said no problem. All my friends said I was just trying to cover all my bases. In truth, I didn't learn much about the liturgy of the Catholic Church, and have always felt ignorant when it comes to ritual. That ignorance led to some uncomfortable, if not embarrassing situations.

At this point, I think I should make it clear that in no way should anyone form opinions, or feel they have learned anything from my religious experiences, opinions, or practices. Certainly I will have enough trouble getting through those proverbial gates, without having led anyone astray.

I have formed certain opinions through my multiple experiences with organized religions. Baptists sing better than Catholics. Blacks have more fun in church than whites. Everyone stretches the rules a little. For instance, I go to confession when I am out of the country, where the priest doesn't understand English.

It would have been impossible for me to not be thrown out of the Catholic Church before Vatican II. Growing up at Cross Creek, we ate fish when they were biting, and steak any time we had it. Old habits die slow. I still go to Protestant services because I enjoy the singing. And no one can compete with the Japanese when it comes to classy funerals.

In the 1980s, I contracted with a German family who were of the old aristocracy that had ruled Germany for centuries. They wanted me to design a theme park. Their ancestors had lived in the same castles since the thirteenth century, and while German titles are not supposed to be in current use, barons and baronesses, counts and countesses are known and respected by the German citizenry.

There is no way one could conceivably describe the infinite space that lies between a Cracker from Cross Creek and a titled German who grew up in a castle with walls twelve feet thick, and with so many rooms that he had never counted them, including a private chapel for the family, complete with a small balcony for the servants.

Throughout my three-year tenure in the land of Beethoven and Bismarck, near the source of the Ruhr, there were daily conflicts of cultures between German aristocracy and Cracker mentality. They were generally resolved without much loss of dignity or temper.

I had learned in South America that if you don't know the language, never do business without an interpreter. So I demanded two interpreters, one to be there when I woke up and stay at my side until three o'clock, the second to come on at two o'clock so they could exchange information and stay on duty until I went to bed.

In addition, my contract was to include having a full-time automobile at my disposal. They had a great public transit system. However, there is nothing like a car in an emergency situation, such as when an American is without toothpaste, or has a sudden urge for a doughnut at three in the morning.

They balked on the car. I insisted. They said you have interpreters with autos. I insisted. They gave in and provided me with one of those little French Citrons with the canvas tops, the vehicle that originated the classic automotive description, "lemon." I asked where the mower blade was. They didn't think my comment was funny.

On Sunday, I accompanied the German family to mass in the town's huge old church. They didn't have heat in the building, and it was colder in the church in July than on a street in Chicago in February. Everyone wore heavy coats. The family pew was behind a huge pillar, making it impossible to see the altar. My interpreter said it didn't matter since the masses were all alike, and even though you couldn't see, one knew what was going on.

I thought I would try a small country church in the village of Voss Vinkle, expecting it to be like the small parishes back home. When I arrived for the evening mass, the men were standing around outside, talking in the manner they do around country churches back home, probably about farming, and local male gossip.

Not knowing anyone, and not wanting to appear too forward, I elected to go inside and meditate until mass started. Inside, everyone was sitting on one side, to the left of the center aisle of the church, possibly, I thought, having something to do with the heat. I selected a seat about half way down, not wanting to appear too bold by sitting up front, or too shy by sitting in the back.

After a moment, I became aware that everyone was looking at me out of the corners of their eyes. Then I noticed that there were no men in church. And on closer observation, I realized that all the women in the area where I had chosen to sit, looked to be in their thirties. The oldest women were in the back, and they were all progressively younger towards the front.

I was contemplating getting up and leaving, when all the men suddenly came in and sat across the aisle on the other side of the church, the oldest to the rear, and the youngest down toward the altar. Simultaneously, the priest came through a side door and started saying mass.

The homily was all in German, and I have never been more self-conscious than throughout that interminable mass, sitting in the young ladies section, on the female side of the church. My German host thought it was hilarious. The little church was following the seating manner they have followed for centuries.

The Baron said, "All the country folk will be gossiping about the American that sat with the young women."

I do not owe any gratitude to Lucille for the Voss Vinkle episode.

Among the barons and baronesses, there was one special lady. She was the Baroness of Holenhofen Castle, a beautiful building of modest size. That is not to say that it was small. When compared with other German castles, it was small, but if it were in England, it would be a large castle. I understand there were nearly fifty Allied officers billeted there following World War II, and even with that much company, it was not necessary for the Baron and his family to move out of the portions of the castle they traditionally occupied.

Holenhofen Castle was surrounded by a sprawling lawn, and bordered by a dense wooded area. It was beautiful and private, if one can call any castle private. The ancient structure dated back to the thirteenth century, and was complete with a tower and twelve foot thick walls. The moat had been partially filled, and converted into a reflection pool, complete with water lilies and two magnificent white swans.

As my friends back at Cross Creek would say, "All in all, a feller would be obliged to be impressed if they was in a place like that."

I had contracted, primarily, with the younger brother who had broken with tradition, and lived in a private home in a nearby town. I was offered a room with a twenty foot ceiling, and medieval armor. It was tempting, but I chose a guesthouse across the moat from the castle.

English was as common at Holenhofen as Spanish is in Miami. The Baron acquired his Ph.D. in New York, and the Baroness, Csilla, was a graduate of Vassar. I am sure the Baroness' name was more complicated, but she introduced herself simply as Csilla. They had two lovely children about eight and ten.

The castle reeked of history and had a feeling of being a part of the earth itself. In the 1980s, Holenhofen was sitting comfortably, only a few kilometers from a very modern Germany. Shiny automobiles murmured in and out of the drive where horse-drawn carriages had traversed for more than five hundred years.

On Sunday afternoons during the summer months, the Holenhofen Beethoven Concert was held in the main ballroom, which provided a sweeping view of the gardens and grounds. It seemed natural to assume that concerts had been a normal happening in that room long before Richard Wagner or Ludwig Beethoven were born. In keeping with the ambience, the guests all wore elegant attire, and were quite naturally residents of other castles. Everyone sat attentively through the first movement of the concert, including the appropriately dressed children.

During the intermission, the men, in groups of three or four, strolled about the grounds, while the ladies sipped champagne and tea. Since I could not understand German, I could not discern whether the ladies gossiped or discussed the arts. However, it was safe to assume that the men discussed business, and therefore, politics.

Although I was treated as a special guest, and occasionally included myself in the events of the moment, Holenhofen was part fairytale and part reality. When I drifted off and became an observer, the Baroness Csilla von Boselager, the First Lady of the castle, drew me back into conversations in English, like any good hostess.

Baroness Boselager was very attractive, comfortably sophisticated, blond, and vivacious. Her enthusiastic Hungarian style reminded one of the Gabor sisters. She loved America, and therefore Pat and I thought she was great. On one social occasion, someone was a little critical of America, and Csilla politely interrupted, "Do you know what I like about America?"

Everyone said, "What?"

Csilla answered, "Skippy Peanut Butt'ah." She thought for a moment and added, "And Aunt Jemima pancakes on Sunday mornings, while reading the funny pap'ahs."

Though most of the guests didn't know what either of her favorites was, they nodded in polite approval. It is amazing how a kind word about America is so appreciated when one is abroad, considering the breadth of the word America, which could mean Beaumont, Texas, San Francisco, Manhattan, or, of course, Cross Creek.

I truly like Germany, and though I do not have any known German ancestry, I am more comfortable there than in any other country on the continent. During the Wild Wald (Wild Forest) project, that lasted more than two years, I returned to the States every four to six weeks during the spring and summer months, and made every effort to be out of Germany before hard winter.

On one of the trips back home, I thought of Csilla's comment about loving peanut butter. I stopped at a supermarket and bought their biggest, two-pound jar of Skippy Crunchy Peanut Butter. The customs agent in Amsterdam opened it, smelled it, and motioned me through. When I crossed into Germany, the agent reopened it, held it up towards the light and rotated it as if he were studying it for color and bouquet, then passed it beneath his nose as if it were Rothschild select vintage.

He shrugged his shoulders and said, "Ja, it is so, American."

I arrived at Holenhofen during the intermission of Beethoven's Symphony Number Five. Because I planned to go to Cologne the next morning, and didn't want to carry my big jar of peanut butter, I elected to quietly give my gift to Csilla at some opportune moment. Without any other option, I took the tissue paper from a new shirt, wrapped it around the jar, and twisted the paper over the top.

The men had returned from the gardens, and were joining the ladies for the second movement, when I entered the ballroom. All the guests were trying to conclude their conversations before being seated. For a brief moment, Csilla was separate from the guests. I thought it was the perfect time to hand her the tissue wrapped jar. As I approached her, she saw me, and said, "Oh, Mr. Glisson, you are back. How nice."

All the guests were moving towards their chairs, so I simply handed her the humble gift and said, "It's something for you."

Although I have a narrow experience with Hungarian ladies, I am convinced one should never expect them to be discreet when it comes to gifts. The Baroness clapped her hands over her head. There was a sudden silence in the room.

She announced in a clear tone, " Everyone, Mr. Glisson has just returned from America! And he has brought me a gift!" She ripped the shirt paper away, and made a cultured squealing sound. "It is peanut butt'ah! What is even more delightful is, it is Crunchy Skippy Peanut Butt'ah!" She held it up in the air as if it was the Singles Trophy at Wimbledon.

There was polite applause, followed by a murmur from the crowd. For a second, I recalled shades of my night landing in Yee-Haw junction, but being the coward that I am on such occasions, I said, "It's from my wife, Pat."

She refused my deception. "No, it is a wonderful gift from you both." The

Baroness of Holenhofen unscrewed the lid, then with unbelievable grace and dignity, she dipped a finger into the content of the jar and tasted it. "Europeans do not know what a magnificent treat they miss not appreciating peanut butt'ah."

Her two children crowded in close, and asked, "What is it, Mother?"

She answered, "It is a special gift. And it is mine."

Csilla was always a gracious lady, even in the most common circumstances. When Pat and my sister came over, they decided to prepare me a southern dinner, complete with corn bread. After considerable effort, they found corn meal in a local store, but needed a square pan to bake it in.

They went across to the castle and knocked on the twelve-foot high doors. A maid answered, but speaking no English, she summoned the lady of the castle.

Csilla came down the stairs and greeted them with, "Do come in."

They apologized for the unannounced visit. "We wanted to borrow a square baking pan for some cornbread."

Csilla said, "Oh, it just happens I have a cornbread pan. It was Mother's, and now I have a use for it."

I am certain there are a very limited number of cornbread pans in Germany, but the Baroness always seemed to be in command of the moment.

Long after the Wild Wald project was complete, Pat and I were surprised to read in the international press that our friend, Baroness Csilla Von Boselager, had been the hero of the 1989 Hungarian uprising. When hundreds of Hungarians climbed the fence into the West German Embassy compound, seeking refuge from the Communists, Csilla chartered a train to Budapest, demanded their free passage, and provided transported all of them to the west. Baroness Csilla Von Boselager was truly a great lady whose spontaneity, intelligence, and charm made the world a better place.

Pat and my Baptist sister, Marjorie, the same sister of the runaway plane episode, came over while there was a lull in the project. It looked like a good time to take a holiday and see some of Europe that we had not previously visited. Pat conveniently had an itinerary somewhere in that filing cabinet she calls her purse.

First, we went to Paris and I was able to spend time in the expressionist galleries at the Louvre. I should have realized there would be a number of religious sites, knowing Pat and my sister. But nevertheless, I agreed to go by Lourdes on the way to Rome. That, of course, is like going from Florida to New York, by way of Denver. We traveled on a rail pass, which provided a chance to see the countryside in southern France.

When we arrived, we got a room in a small hotel teetering on the side of a steep hill. Our room was on the second floor, with a lavatory, but no toilet. The communal toilet was at the opposite end of the building, precariously attached to the siding that was pulling away from the building, causing a screeching sound when anyone was in the minuscule enclosure. There was nothing but a hundred feet of air between it and the bottom of the hill. My sister decided that the first miracle we witnessed in Lourdes was that, although guests regularly used it, no one had gotten killed.

We went to the grotto, and were truly moved by the sanctity of the place. However, my wife Pat got sick at Lourdes while others were being miraculously cured. She recovered shortly after we departed for Rome.

Between Pat, my sister, and the ever-present Lucille, I should have known things would not follow the course I anticipated. Under the illusion that the vacation was primarily centered around European art, we arrived in Rome. (I had proclaimed it the chaotic capital of the world on a previous visit.) Our son, Nick, had arranged for us to stay in a hotel near the Vatican.

As soon as we settled in, Pat mentioned that Nick had also arranged for me to meet an official at the Vatican who would possibly get us seats at the public audience held by the Pope on Wednesday. This was way over my expectations. Although I had been to Washington and London, I had never made an effort to see the President or the Queen. Balking was no good; I was clearly outnumbered. With Lucille's prompting, my Baptist sister said that I should do it just for Pat. It was clear to me that I was surrounded by bossy women, including, Lucille.

Normally, imposing structures do not frighten me, but the Vatican is magnificent and authoritative. I approached one of the Swiss Guards posted just outside the entrance, where the right-hand colonnade joins the main structure. He was regal in his light orange and navy blue striped uniform, topped off with a jaunty beret and a spear.

I said, "My wife, Pat, said I was supposed to see Monsignor McGee."

He said, "An appointment with whom, sir?"

I repeated, "Monsignor McGee."

"If you will follow me, sir, I will direct you."

As we went inside, I felt like a kid following a drum major in a Fourth of July parade. He directed me to a man standing behind a security desk. I told the man that I was J.T. Glisson from America. I didn't think mentioning Cross Creek would be of any value. I stated that my son had told my wife that his friend, a fellow priest in Washington, D.C., had arranged for me to speak to a Monsignor McGee.

The man asked to see my passport, then handed it to another official who gave me a form that included the address of the hotel we were in and the number in our party. He came back, returned my passport, gave me a pass, and then said, "Monsignor McGee is expecting you. If you would take the stairs just inside and to the right, you will come out into a courtyard. Then take the first door to the right, and it will lead you directly to the Monsignor's office."

The stairs were like something in a dream that might lead to the Pearly Gates.

They were so narrow that if one met someone coming down, they couldn't pass. The arched ceiling was low, causing me to stoop to avoid touching it. Looking up from the bottom, they appeared to go to infinity. Actually, they did extend up to what I would estimate to be six or seven normal stories. Apparently, people were not very tall when Bernini designed the building.

Finally, reaching the top, I stepped out onto a patio that was on ground level. I couldn't believe I had climbed so high and was still on the ground. I turned to the right and entered the door.

A priest greeted me with a warm smile and said, "I have been expecting you. In fact, I just finished talking to your friend, Father Milt Jordan, in Washington." Monsignor McGee showed me around his office and explained that the window was the one the Pope appeared in occasionally to greet the throngs that gathered in St. Peter's Square below.

I looked out the window, hoping Lucille would take note of her charge in such a hallowed setting. The monsignor told me he was the master of ceremonies for the Pope, and would have a messenger deliver our tickets to my hotel for front row seats at the audience the following day.

Before he let me go, he said, "If for any for reason you don't get to meet the Pontiff, come back and I will arrange an alternative."

I strutted down the long stairs and back to the hotel, where I told the women in my entourage that I had arranged everything. They wanted details, but I brushed them aside with a simple, "It was nothing."

The next afternoon, a crowd, usually estimated to be a quarter million, gathered in the piazza—St. Peters' Square. It was packed with pilgrimages from all over the world. Marjorie, Pat and I were escorted to our places near the podium. When the Pope appeared with Monsignor McGee at his side, I have never felt such a state of joy as emerged from that gathering.

Monsignor McGee stepped to the microphone, and began announcing the visitors that had come to have a public audience with the head of their church. He began with, "His Holiness welcomes the pilgrimage from San Palo, Brazil." A mighty cheer went up from a section near the back of the throng. The monsignor continued, "And His Holiness would like to extend his welcome to the pilgrimage from Stuttgart." A roar of cheers went up from another area. He continued to announce the pilgrimages from great cities all over the world. And each time, a mighty cheer rose from a distinct area the crowd cheered and the Pontiff waved in their direction. We were traumatized by the exuberance following each announcement.

Then totally unexpectedly, Monsignor McGee said, "And His Holiness would especially like to welcome the pilgrimage from St. Augustine's in Gainesville, Florida."

For the first time in my life, I was petrified. My mouth fell open. He was introducing Pat, Marjorie and me. We sat frozen, like the stone statues around the top of the colonnades. The Pontiff looked in one area of the crowd, and then another. At one point, he looked directly to where we were standing. The three stooges just stood there. There was no cheer. It was possibly the quietest moment in the history of Rome. Finally, Monsignor McGee went on to the next pilgrimage.

When it was over, we staggered back to the hotel. Lucille couldn't resist. She said that it had been an historical day. We had been the quietest Glissons in the family's entire history.

Pat soon recovered, and told me, "You said that Monsignor McGee said if we didn't get to meet the Pope, for you to come back and he would make alternate arrangements."

I said, "Oh, no! I am not going back to say, 'This is dumb-dumb, who froze at the public audience. Monsignor, would you ask Pope John Paul II to ask the three dodos from Gainesville, Florida, to welcome us again?'"

I lost again. The next day, I went back over and asked the Swiss guard if I could see Monsignor McGee. I climbed the stairs again and went to the monsignor's office.

He said, "Where were you? I looked all over and could not find you. I knew you had seats near the podium."

I said, "We were the three pale faces with our mouths hanging open."

He laughed. "Well, it is short notice, but I can arrange something better."

He explained that the Pope is the Bishop of Rome, and part of his duties is to say mass at one of the hundreds of parishes in Rome every Sunday. He said it was not customary to have any outside visitors, but he would arrange a special exception in our case.

He said that the security police arranged the entire affair, and no one knew which parish the Pope would visit until about an hour before he would arrive there. We were to wait at our hotel on Sunday, and a special messenger would bring our passes. We should take a taxi and go immediately to the address on the passes.

The messenger arrived, and we grabbed a cab and went to a small village in the outskirts of Rome. When we arrived, Pope John Paul was inside the local school, visiting with the children. From all the laughter we heard, they must have had a marvelous time. In fact, the Pope was late for the mass because he stayed longer than expected with the children.

The mass was held outdoors, and the people, recognizing we were strangers, warmly welcomed us and seated us on the front row. Pat and I received Holy Communion from the Pope. When I stood inches from the head of the Catholic Church, we looked directly into each other's eyes. I saw only humility, love, and compassion.

When it was over, Pat and I walked back to the bus stop, lost in our own thoughts. I had never felt so holy in my life; then I discovered I didn't have any money. Pat didn't have any money, either. The bus came, we got on, wondering what they do to people in Italy who do not pay their fares on public buses. When we sneaked off, we were the two holiest crooks in Rome.

Chapter 15

THE LAST HOUSE IN HENSCRATCH

The best things in life do not necessarily happen in exotic, faraway places. In fact, I cannot remember a time I enjoyed more than the time my turkey-hunting friends tried to save an outhouse for posterity.

As the years slipped by, the original Miami-artists-turned-turkey-hunters gradually migrated to other jobs in other cities across the country. Only my friend, Russ Smiley, remained in Miami. However, the artistic turkey hunters' love of hunting in the Everglades never diminished.

Each year, they individually flew down to Miami, rented a car, and met in the Everglades. For the next seven days, they stayed in simple tents, slept in sleeping bags, turkey hunted, and told exaggerated stories of their successes in past years. Naturally, no one remembered any successes except his own. The annual hunt became a tradition for all of us. It was like the Yuletide reading of Dickens' Christmas Carol, or the passion play at Easter. We had our cast of characters, and generally followed the same script.

Russ Smiley, six foot two inches tall, and good-natured, liked to hunt early and late. And although I hate to admit it, he is a better hunter than I. You remember, Russ was the man who gave me my first job as a turkey-hunting artist in 1951. He was the organizer, and generally the un-elected leader of the hunt.

Tom Gaskin was the senior citizen, and general authority on all matters pertaining to the Everglades, philosophy, and local history. Tom was the only one of the group that was not a professional artist, although he was more creative than most of us. He had been born in the edge of the 'Glades, and had grown up learning the ways of backwoods Crackers and Seminole Indians. Other than a stint at the University, he had spent his life in the Fish Eating Creek Area on the northern perimeter of the Everglades.

He was an artist in his own right. He recognized the beauty of the abstract shapes of cypress knees (appendages that grow up from the roots of cypresses). He was the first to peel them and sell them to tourists. Tom even built a cypress knee museum on U.S. Highway 27 that is still open today.

Tom Gaskin's turkey calls are the best I have ever used. Although unconventional, he was gentleman, a naturalist, and a conservationist. Until this day, I do not know anyone that ever saw Tom wearing shoes. We all respected his opinion, but loved to get him riled when we displayed our ignorance of history and tradition. There is no one I respected more than Tom Gaskin, and was honored when he referred to me as a friend.

When the water was low, we usually hunted in the area known as Big Cypress. When the water was high, we hunted near Tom's home in the, Likes Brothers Management Area, which was the source of Fish Eating Creek. Although there were deer, wild hogs, and turkeys, we were only interested in the turkeys.

The open woods west of U.S. 27 extended more than 20 miles, before crossing State Road 31. Traveling cross-country in a Jeep, it seemed endless. It is the only place in Florida that I have ever been lost. It consists of flat savannas, which are covered with scrawny scrub palmettos, and wiregrass that grows only about a foot high. Little ponds are spaced about a mile apart, containing skinny cypress trees called pond cypresses, and occasionally, a few small live oaks. Ten miles in any direction looks the same.

In all that vast space, there is only one recognizable landmark. It is a humble, abandoned outhouse, sitting like a monument in the center of the vast open space. When we hunted in the Fish Eating Creek Area, the outhouse was the gathering place. It was also the only place of reference we had for other locations in the preserve. We would describe a place where we found turkey tracks as three miles northeast of the outhouse. Or, we are going to hunt near the third pond west by northwest of the outhouse.

Most importantly, it was the one point where we could pick up the dim path to find our way out. In the morning, we would break camp and tell our buddies we will meet you at the toilet. Once we were there, we planned our day's hunting, and split up in pairs to the locations we believed we would find a turkey.

When the sun dropped to the horizon, we met back at the outhouse. Everyone unloaded their guns and secured them in the Jeeps. Then it was time to have a drink, and lie about why we didn't get a turkey. On the rare occasion when someone was lucky, we had to listen to every detail of how the great hunter had outwitted the bird and had hit it with an almost impossible shot. The only exception was Tom Gaskin who got more birds than the rest of us combined.

Tom told a story like the fishermen back at Cross Creek, a little bit at a time. He usually started by getting out his whittling knife, pausing, and beginning with, "Well, fellers, I called and waited, called again, and that old gobbler answered. Then he let the hens come first, but I waited, and when he was in close range, I shot him in the head so the shot wouldn't ruin the meat." Everyone agreed that Tom was a great storyteller, but he missed the key ingredient when it came to turkey stories; he left out the exaggeration.

Bob Esslinger, a cartoonist, was our camp cook. He had strict rules; we gave him our share of the cost and he bought the food. He didn't take any lip, and he didn't do dishes. And even though the food was great, it would have been inadvisable for anyone to make suggestions about his cooking. Bob was always in a good mood, and I looked forward to hearing him play the guitar.

Everyone is a character when they have room to be, and there is more than enough room in the Everglades. The Miami Artist Turkey Hunters had more than its share of characters.

One evening, when we had all gathered around the outhouse and passed the bottle, one of our charter members, whom I referred to as "Mister-What's-His-Name," was sitting in the old outhouse. Jeeps are notoriously uncomfortable to lean on, or for casual sitting, so the toilet was the preferred seat in the area. The door and the floor had rotted away years before, but the seat was still intact. Mister-What's-His-Name was sitting in there, looking like his mind was a million miles away.

I asked, "Why do you look so philosophical?"

He looked as if I had broken a trance. He said, "Glisson, I was just thinking. I live on Long Island. I get up before daylight most of the year, and catch a train into Manhattan. I grab a cab to my office, work eight hours, and sometimes ten or twelve hours. Neither rain, snow, pot holes, nor traffic keep me from my drawing board, or client conferences."

Everyone stopped their conversations to listen to his narrative. He continued, "Frequently, I go in and work on Saturdays. Sundays consist of "honey dos," and well-earned rest. Then I am back on Mondays for another week."

He paused, then continued, "But! Once a year, I take my two- thousand-dollar shotguns, wear my L.L. Bean hunting clothes, and fly first class to Miami. I rent a car and drive out here to turkey hunt. And most years, I don't even kill a turkey. And to answer your question, I believe you asked what I was thinking about, I was wondering if there is not something wrong with my priorities. Here I am, sitting in what most of the world calls a s--- house, in the middle of nowhere, drinking twelve-year-old single malt Scotch from a plastic cup." He feigned a sincere expression. "I ask you, Glisson, am I crazy? Perhaps we all are."

Tom Gaskin, a man who never missed an opportunity to philosophize when the door was opened, stepped forward. Pointing first at Mister-What's-His-Name, and then gesturing at all of us, he opened with, "You fellers never really look at what you are seeing, and fail to appreciate the things you already know."

Someone said, barely audibly, "Tom is fixing to tell us." Tom ignored the remark. "You fellers have been here many times, and not one of you knows where you are."

We asked, "Where are we, Tom? We don't see anything higher than our knees for several miles, but a couple of ponds."

"Gentlemen, you are standing in the middle of Henscratch, Florida." He pointed north, and said, "The main street used to start up there a ways, and go a hundred yards past here. I was born in a house right over there, off the main street. We had a blacksmith shop, two general stores, an apothecary, two rooming houses, and a post office. And you fellers think you are in the middle of nowhere."

We hung our heads in shame. Tom wasn't finished. "That old outhouse you are making fun of is the last house in Henscratch, Florida. It is as much a part of *americana* as the Washington Monument. It is functionally designed, utilitarian, and it has a pitched roof. It also has the required quarter moon, representing the supernatural origin of lunar mysticism. At the time this structure was built, over 90 percent of American homes had one." He paused for effect, "Gentleman, what you are looking at, and making fun of, is pure *americana*."

We were all moved. Someone said, "And it's a miracle it ain't burned in one of the woods fires."

Someone else said, "It ought to be preserved." Of course, the few drinks had nothing to do with the sentimentality, but everyone agreed it was necessary to save one of the last relics of our American heritage.

So saying, we all got around the outhouse, lifted it straight up, and set it on Russ's Jeep. It fit like it and the Jeep were made for each other. Since there was no floor left in the outhouse, there was room for Russ to sit in front of the seat. We were so pleased with ourselves, that we decided we should transport it with proper dignity and respect. Two Jeeps formed a forward honor guard, and the other two Jeeps, a rear guard. We moved out at a slow pace, to keep it from falling off over the rough terrain.

About five miles from the outhouse's original site, the Game Department had a check station where they searched the vehicles coming in and out, for illegal game. They checked each vehicle carefully. When they came to the Jeep with the outhouse on it, they solemnly checked it and waved it through as if an outhouse came through the check station every few minutes. It was necessary to proceed down U.S. 27 for four or five miles, using our headlights in the fog. And though there was some traffic, we continued as a convoy, with the dignity worthy of the American icon we were transporting

Tom Gaskin's wife was one of the nicest ladies I have ever met. She was certainly one of the most pleasant and patient, because Tom was the kind of man that if he met three or four hunters in the woods, and he liked them, he would invite them home for dinner. She told me he had brought dinner guests home as

late as nine o'clock. Mrs. Gaskin would treat them with the respect due royal visitors.

We pulled off the highway, into Tom's yard. I suppose we thought she would congratulate us for our contribution to American history. That was not to be.

She came out of the house, looked at the outhouse, and said loud and clear, "Tom Gaskin, get that thing out of my yard! And I mean right now!"

We all tried to intercede for Tom and *americana.* We tried historical significance, and we tried architectural heritage. Mrs. Gaskin was not impressed.

She repeated, "Tom, you have drug everything you found in the woods into my yard, but you have gone too far. Get it out!"

There was nothing left to do, but to try an orderly retreat. We asked if we could leave it there for the night, and then take it back where we got it. We promised it would be gone before daylight. She relented a little.

"O.K. But if that thing is in my yard when the sun comes up in the morning, I am going to burn it, and whatever it is sitting on."

So much for *americana.*

The next morning, at five o'clock, we filed out of Mrs. Gaskin's yard—the honor guard in the lead, the Jeep with the outhouse and the rearguard. The fog was bad, but we made it back down U.S. 27 to the check station. The officials looked it over, inside and out, and waved it through. We proceeded to the original outhouse site. Then we lifted it off the Jeep, and set it back in the exact spot where it had sat since before any of us were born. Having finished properly replacing it without disturbing a blade of grass we all dispersed for the day's turkey hunt.

That evening, we gathered back at the outhouse and began to secure our guns.

Esslinger said, "It's kinda nice having it back. It provided a certain ambience that wouldn't be the same without it."

Two Jeeps that were not part of our group, pulled up and stopped. They could not have been more emotional if we had a flying saucer parked there.

One jumped out, and said, "Where did you guys find the toilet? It sure as hell weren't there last night! We drove all over these woods, 'til after midnight, looking for it, 'cause that toilet is the only landmark we knew to find our way out."

We all knew what had happened. Russ said, "Fellers, it has been there where it is sitting as long as I can remember."

One of the hunters said, "It weren't there last night."

Tom asked, "What were you fellers drinking?"

The driver said, "It weren't the liquor. Th' blame thing just plain disappeared."

We said it was here yesterday after we finished hunting, and it was here this morning. They drove off, swearing and arguing with one another.

We had a good laugh, and Bob Esslinger proposed a toast. We raised our glasses. "Here is to *americana* – to the last house in Henscratch and the only outhouse in America that ever had a night out."

Chapter 16

WEST OF KEY WEST

There was never a time that I needed and appreciated my guardian angel more than in the summer of 1984. I was fishing off Key West, when my time and luck suddenly ran out. Looking back on that fateful day, I have no choice but to give Lucille, and the Power she represents, credit for my survival.

In the spring of '83, Hollywood descended on Cross Creek. The rumors were Universal International was doing a movie based on Marjorie Kinnan Rawlings' bestseller, *Cross Creek*. Locally, there was little or no excitement, since the book did not lend itself to the Cracker version of what a movie should be. The announcement caused me to remember my dad's comment about the movie business.

He said, "Them Hollywood people can take something that is really great and make it into something insignificant. And they can take something measly and make it into something bigger than all creation."

My first inclination was to avoid the film makers as much as possible. I unfairly assumed they would do a Malibu Beach version of my beloved birthplace, with no respect for the local residents, or the area. I was wrong, and in time, I did become involved.

A few weeks after they started production on the film, Pat and I accepted an invitation to a dinner party at the Marjorie Rawlings house. Her house is now a part of the State Park system. We didn't expect there would be any connection between the dinner party and the film being shot four miles south, on the shore of Orange Lake.

Rip Torn, one of the actors in the film, was among the guests and, to my surprise, did not reflect any of the stereotypes of Hollywood. In fact, he seemed comfortable in the backwoods environment. We talked about fishing, hunting, and the small town where he grew up in Texas. Using an old Cracker expression, he seemed to be an all right kind of feller. He is a gentleman, and it seemed unfair to hold one actor responsible for all the grievances directed toward the film industry.

So, I thoroughly enjoyed the evening, and the delightful dinner the hostess had prepared. When the hour was late, Pat and I thanked our hostess, and sincerely wished Mr. Torn success. He invited us over to the set, and I said thanks, but I didn't think so. We said goodbye.

A week later, Rip called and asked if he could stop over at my house for a short visit. I, of course, said yes. After the usual niceties, he said he would like me to do him a favor. He wanted me to look at the props that had been collected for his role in *Cross Creek*. I agreed on the condition that it be at a time when everyone else would be off the set.

We met at the old Drew residence, where he was staying, late the following afternoon. We discussed local fishing and hunting, while we strolled down through Cane Hammock road through the orange grove that led to the set. On the edge of the lake, the carpenters had constructed a dock, and a small cottage that represented the former home of Mrs. Rawlings. A boat lay upside down, near the dock.

Rip said, "J.T., that is the boat they got for me. I'm playing a local character who fished and hunted here on the lakes in the '30's. What do you think?"

I didn't realize how important the authenticity of props were to an actor, and particularly, to Rip Torn. So I gave him one of our overstated Cracker answers. "If the Indians came charging down from the mountains to attack a wagon train, riding Harley Davidson motorcycles, it would be as authentic as that boat would have been at Cross Creek in the '30s."

I discovered something I didn't know about my new friend. He can disapprove of something with more cavalier expressions, without a single word of profanity, than anyone I have ever known.

His questions were short and to the point. "Specifically what is wrong with it?"

I said, "It was designed for saltwater. It is not made of cypress. It has plywood incorporated in its construction and we didn't have plywood back then. Also, it has a transom for a large outboard motor. Cross Creek fishermen never saw a boat shaped like that."

Rip is a man of action. "Where can we get an authentic boat?"

I said I didn't know because all the fishermen had converted to plywood, and acquired small outboards in the late '40's.

He continued, "Where are the old boats?"

"The fishermen gave them to cattlemen to use for feed troughs," I answered.

"Who can build one now?"

I told him, "I cannot think of anyone that isn't dead, except me."

He was unrelenting, "When can you start?"

I didn't know if I had time, or would want to build one of the old boats.

Rip ignored my remarks. He asked, "Where can we get the kind of lumber you used on the local boats back then?"

I explained that they were made of cypress, and the only place I knew was a small mill down in the big scrub at Eureka. Local Crackers had pulled logs from the river bottom, where some sank when the loggers tried to float them to the big mills in the late nineteenth century. In addition, I told him the sawmill operator was independent, and I didn't know if he would cut boat lumber, even if we asked.

Rip said, "Can we go the first thing in the morning?"

I do not remember if I told him I would build the boat. It did occur to me that it would be kind of sporting to build one for old time's sake.

The next morning, Rip came to my house early. We set out to the big scrub to get cypress to build the boat. I told Rip, "If we rushed the mill owner, he will run us off."

Rip said they were the same way in Texas, and assured me if it became a contest of patience, we would win and get our boat lumber.

After seven hours of hunkering, whittling, and telling Florida and Texas fishing and snake stories, the operator agreed to cut our lumber. We hauled it home on my boat trailer, with no taillights.

For the next two days and nights, Rip dodged off the set any time he was not needed in a scene, and we built and antiqued it to make it authentic-looking to the boats of the late '30s. We named it the *Bull Gator,* and hauled it over to the set. Rip arranged a lease agreement, equal to the cost of the material, that gave us exclusive ownership when the film was finished. We thoroughly enjoyed building the boat.

Shortly after we delivered it, we had seventeen inches of rain, resulting in a flood. Rip said the director told him the *Bull Gator* was invaluable in scenes that were originally supposed to be shot on dry land.

When the film was finished, Rip had become a personal friend and in many ways, a permanent part of Cross Creek. When he was leaving, he promised to come back so we could catch up on the fishing we missed while they were shooting the film.

We were pleased when he was nominated for an Academy Award for his performance in *Cross Creek.*

Just before the awards were to be presented, he called, and said, "J.T., I am ready to take you up on the fishing." I said that fish were not biting in the local lakes, but I had been hankering to go fishing in my favorite spot off Key West. He said, "That sounds great. I'll be down tomorrow."

The next morning, he arrived in a great mood, and we set out for the seven-hour drive to Key West. There is no time in a man's life when he is in a better mood, and more optimistic, than when he is going fishing. I discovered that the awards ceremony was only two days away. That left us only one day fishing. Rip said that he had wanted to get away, so that he would not have to explain to everyone that there were several nominations, and that he didn't care to speculate on the final selection. He assured me one day's fishing was worth the trip.

Come sunup the next morning, we were in a Boston Whaler with a forty-horse Mercury motor, cruising to Sand Key Reef, six miles southeast of Key West. We caught barracudas, big and small. Rip proved to be a master with spinning tackle. He had one on that came out of the water and jumped over the boat, landing on the opposite side. He landed him. In addition, we caught a humongous jack.

Coming in at sundown, we agreed life did not get better than that. We had a fine seafood dinner, and went back to the hotel. Rip speculated on the possibility of going out fishing before his 9:00 a.m. flight. I didn't think so. It was the only flight out of Key West that day.

Once back in New York, Rip would join his family and fly to Houston to pick up his mother. Then, they would all be off to Los Angeles and the Awards. I had met some of his family, and talked to others on the phone. I didn't want to be a partner in causing him and his family to miss the Academy Awards. With mixed emotions, he caught the flight, leaving some good fishing. To comfort him, I mumbled something to the effect that I would not go back fishing myself.

Out of loyalty to a fishing friend, and a half-hearted promise, I convinced myself to not go fishing. Feeling noble, I decided to do a watercolor of one of the magnificent old houses in Key West. I gathered my watercolors and set up in a comfortable spot beneath a huge banyan tree. The watercolor went well. However, I found myself rushing it.

In spite of my efforts to banish it, there was one thought that repeatedly came into my mind: all those fish out in that blue green water, waiting to be caught. I felt like an alcoholic, inventorying stock in a liquor store. Shortly after three o'clock, I had a willpower meltdown. I picked up my supplies and headed for the boat rental dock.

Lucille suddenly appeared and said, "You know better than going fishing out in the ocean, alone, and you promised you would not."

The dock master informed me there would be other sport fishermen going out, a half mile past the last channel marker on the Gulf side. All I had to do was stay near them, and I would not be alone. After all, I am a competent boat operator with many hours of experience. Furthermore, I had said I would not go back to where Rip and I had been fishing, which was in the Atlantic. The Gulf was different. Therefore, I was keeping my promise. I told Lucille to stay at the dock, and I cast off.

I went around to the Gulf side and entered the west channel. The steering was a little loose and caused the boat to pull to the left, making it necessary to manually hold it on course. I planned to tell the rental service it needed tightening, but it was not serious at the moment. A half-mile past the last channel marker, I saw five boats fishing in a small area. Anchoring near them, I discovered that in my haste to get underway, I didn't bring any cut bait. I had chum, but nothing with which to catch the first fish. A half hour passed before I dipped a short piece of my shoelace in the chum and enticed a small grunt to bite it.

I put all my chum into the water, and cast my line. It didn't get to the bottom before a five-pound red snapper was on the line. The next cast was the same. My expertise, and more likely the chum, was fantastic. None of the other boats were catching anything.

I got a big fish on that took several minutes to land. While I was getting it off, three of the boats cranked and headed in toward Key West. No matter. I continued fishing.

The sun was twenty minutes high when the last two boats pulled anchor and headed in. The water was calm, with only ground swells. The surface was as smooth as glass. Ten or fifteen minutes wouldn't make any difference.

After catching several fish in fast succession, I reluctantly hauled in the anchor. Twilight is very short at that latitude. With the throttle full open, I leaned back in the seat to enjoy the ride in, comforted that I would arrive before it was totally dark.

There was no need to secure the fish that I had dropped into the boat. The ground swells were like the roller coaster in a children's park. I was a happy man. I had a boatload of fish. The weather was perfect. It had been a great day, and would culminate with a dinner at my favorite restaurant, topped off with a large serving of Key Lime pie. After a shower and a good night's sleep, I would casually drive home the next day. Any thoughts of shame for telling Rip I would not go fishing had vanished. In fact, I knew ultimately I would brag to him about my success.

The boat glided along at about thirty-five knots, running perfectly. Suddenly, the lid blew off the ice chest, causing me to release the wheel for a split second, and grab for the lid. There was a crashing sound, and I found myself flying through the air. I then hit the water, and sank like a rock. I was afraid to surface because if the boat didn't sink, and the motor was still running I didn't want to get sliced up by the propeller.

After a minute, there was no choice. I had to surface for air, hoping the propeller wouldn't get me. I expected to see the boat upside down, and seat cushions and gas tanks floating around me. I popped up and couldn't believe it. There was nothing. No boat, no debris.

Treading water, I turned, and a hundred fifty yards to the north, the boat was puttering along at about two miles an hour. Obviously, the motor had swung to a full right angle, causing the boat to summersault. It had thrown me out, and came down right side up. As I was catapulted out, a reflex reaction caused my left hand, which was still on the throttle, to pull it to idle, leaving the motor in gear.

I was in trouble, big trouble. The tide was going out. There were no channel markers to hold onto. There was nothing but the open Gulf of Mexico. No one was expecting me back.

With as much respect as I could invoke, I implored Lucille, "I need your help! Now!"

Taking my shoes off made it easier to tread water. In service, they taught us that if you went down at sea, you could survive for many hours by relaxing and floating with your face in the water. Only when it was absolutely necessary should you raise your head to exhale and inhale as deeply as possible. It could be hours before an airplane or boat might spot me.

I remembered a couple, wearing life jackets who spent two days and nights in the Gulf before they were rescued. They said that the worst part of their ordeal had been being tortured by needlefish constantly picking at them.

When I raised my head the second time, I was facing the boat. It seemed nearer. I went over Lucille's head. I asked God to help me to get back to that boat.

The boat was definitely running in a curving direction. I watched it for another minute, and was sure it was moving in a wide circle. This was no time to make another mistake. There was a chance I might make it to the boat. Watching it slowly arching, I figured the point it would come closest to me would necessitate swimming in the opposite direction from the boats present position.

It is amazing how your brain will tell you one thing, and your impulses another. In spite of what I knew I should do, I wanted to swim directly toward the boat. I repeatedly had to convince myself. I knew if there would be any chance of intersecting with the boat as it went by, it would be by swimming in the opposite direction.

Thankfully, the gear and throttle were on the side I hoped to approach. The urge to hurry was almost uncontrollable. Several times, I had to force myself to slow down. My progress was slow and laborious at first, but after removing my long sleeved shirt, swimming was easier. Down in the water, all I could see on land was a red light, blinking on a water tower in Key West. From time to time, I tread-water and glanced at the boat moving quietly to my left. After swimming for fifteen or twenty minutes, which seemed like eternity, I summoned a last minute spurt of energy, converged with the boat, reached up and pulled the throttle out of gear.

It was impossible to climb directly in, I was too tired to lift myself up over the gunwale. I worked around to the stern, and attempted to climb up on the motor to get into the boat. I could not do it. I was exhausted.

Lucille said, "You have made it this far. Take your time, rest."

I held there for five or more minutes, and finally crawled into the boat.

I was overwhelmed. There was an absolute feeling of peace, combined with gratitude, and the joy that comes with security. Looking up at the millions of stars extending a billion light years from Key West, I said, "Thank you, God, and thanks for Lucille. Thank you, Lucille, and all guardian angels everywhere."

In a few short minutes, Lucille had been transformed from a bossy advisor, a matriarch, a source of conscience, and an occasional nag, to a friend, and an indispensable part of my life.

The centrifugal force of the boat flipping had held everything in place, including the fish and life cushions. I drove the boat back to the marina, tied it up, picked up my spinning rod, got into my car, and headed up the Keys in the direction of home. Nothing seemed more important than that.

During the seven and a half hour drive, I did some serious thinking. First of all, I thought I should pay more attention to Lucille. And after swimming around in the Gulf, sitting in a rocking chair seemed nice. (After a little more thought, I discarded that one.)

I could buy another airplane. I rejected that thought because although I like to think I have kept up with the times, I am, as a matter of fact, from another era. Today, the skies over Florida are congested with electronically equipped aircraft that are faster, and less forgiving. My grandchildren would call my kind of airplanes dinosaurs, if they knew what a Stearman or a Luscombe was.

One thing was certain, if I didn't come up with something, Lucille would.

Two and a half hours later, I passed the Miami Airport, and about eleven o'clock, passed Yeehaw Junction. My experience there had been a little hairy, but fun. Living on, what some would consider, the edge had made life exciting. However, there was no denying it. I couldn't have done it without a guardian angel. And any other angel except Lucille would have dumped me after the Chitose River, or the Cypress Gardens episode.

All Lucille wanted was gratitude. So, gratitude was what I would give. The more I thought about it, I had been downright selfish, always giving myself credit for my survival. The time had come to show my respect, and graduate.

"Thank you, Lucille." I said it louder, "I thank you, Lucille. You are most kind. And I thank you!"

She seemed happy.

It is amazing what one can do when they have a good relationship with their guardian angel. A few weeks after the Key West dunking, I bought an ultralight. It was green, so Pat and all my neighbors in Evinston and Cross Creek called it *Kermit*. It is not necessary to fly high enough to mingle with the modern aircraft that fly over our area, so I confined myself to a nine hundred foot ceiling.

People say that I talked to myself when I flew *Kermit*. I was not talking to myself. I talked to Lucille. When I flew between two trees, I said, "Thank you, Lucille." When I passed over the big gators in Orange Lake, I said, "Thank you, Lucille." And when I landed, and rolled the nose wheel through fresh cow do-do, I still say, "Thank you, Lucille."

EPILOGUE

Alas, it appears that this prolonged effort to convince Lucille to continue as my guardian angel has come to naught. She now has a list similar to a Manhattan phone directory. Her revised list is longer than the incidents included in this chronicle.

Thankfully, it has caused her to extend her deadline temporally. I have one thing in my favor: everyday I am confronted with indisputable evidence that I am in an accelerated age mode. I avoid using the word, "old."

I gave up my airplanes and have bought a Catalina Cruiser sailboat. And even though I have not promised, Lucille assumes that there will be no blue water sailing—however, somewhere in the recesses of my mind, I have always wanted to circle the Caribbean. It is only a thought, but with nitroglycerin pills and *El Nino*—who knows?